LOST NOW FOUND

FREEDOM FROM ADDICTION

BY GEROD STURGIS

Lost Now Found – Freedom from Addiction

Scripture quotations are taken from the King James Version, New King James Version, New International Version, NASB, and THE MESSAGE Version of the Bible.

Vision Runners LLC is in collaboration with G-Rod and Stephani Sturgis' 501c3 corporation called Lost Now Found (LNF), a ministry department of A.C.T. International, whose mission is reaching the LOST through entertainment to share the Gospel of Jesus, and walking with them in order for them to FIND, and carry out their God-given purposes in life.

Vision Runner LLC
Adrian, MI 49221
www.GerodSturgis.com
wearevisionrunners@gmail.com
Graphics by Phillip Hammond of Bora Productions

Print ISBN: 978-1-7347871-1-5
Digital eBook ISBN: 978-1-7347871-2-2
Audiobook ISBN: 978-1-7347871-3-9

Dedication

I made a vow to God that if he would deliver me from drugs and alcohol, and if he would save me, that I promised I would share my testimony to the world! So, I would like to dedicate the first book I've ever written to the Triune God who made it all possible! My Mother, who went on to be with the Lord on 11/19/17. She pushed me to write my book she always used to say, "son the whole world needs to hear your story, it's time to write about it." We were actually writing our books simultaneously and pushing each other to finish. My Leaders, Pastor Claude and Rosa Bevier, who helped disciple me and strengthen me to learn God's Word, and to pray and confess His Word faithfully! The whole Restore World Church in Adrian, MI. Apostle Ivory and Evelyn Hopkins, and Pastor Levin and Rose Bailey. My friend L.G Wise and Suzanne and so many more. All of the Prayers and Positive words that I received from so many friends and family as I was writing this book. I've been to so many funerals and spoke with so many love ones young and old who lost love ones due to this demonic spirit of addiction. This book is dedicated to you! To help prevent dark secrets of those who battle with failure and rejection, who may be thinking of suicide, homicide, O.D. or any other type of abuse, because they may not know how to cope and think that alcohol or drugs will fix it. Last but not least to my beautiful Wife Stephani, who would stay up with me countless nights to get this out! Who edited, formatted, and structured it to make sure that I emptied myself. She would see the pain on my face every time I would hear of another drug overdose on the news, or see it on my timeline, or get another phone call, and she would push me from out my pain and say, "They need you, they're waiting on you. Finish the book!"

Table of Contents

Foreword

It's been 29 years since my conversion and my acceptance of Jesus Christ as my Lord and personal savior. Now a Husband, Father, Grandfather, Pastor and Spiritual Father to many; oftentimes people see someone that is successful and think that perhaps they were raised in a great environment and that's why they are so successful. This was not my story at all! I know what it is to grow up in an adverse environment and experience pain and suffering. I also know what it is to overcome so many seemingly insurmountable obstacles such as Gang violence, incarceration throughout my juvenile years, substance abuse, Cocaine addiction and more. My past and background have helped to shape me to see that God's love and grace can change anyone!

Because of this, I believe that God has a plan and a purpose for every person's life that comes through the womb. Not One person is created without purpose and personal significance. Secondly, I also believe that God strategically places individuals in relationships with others who are instrumental for their life success. That is the case when it comes to me and Gerod Sturgis. I by the Grace of God, have become an accomplished gospel hip hop artists having opportunity to influence and to meet many other gospel hip-hop artist, and this common interest is what God used to connect Gerod and I together for a lifetime.

Since our initial connection my role in Gerod's life has shifted from a music industry colleague to becoming his Pastor now for 12 years. This has given me a more personal perspective on his transformation as a Man. It's amazing to not just read his story of how he overcame addiction, violence, and even death, but it's even more fascinating when you know the person and you have seen them fight the good fight of faith to win in the arena of life even when the cards that were dealt to them were not sufficient or favorable for them to win. I remember meeting him years ago at the home of one of gospel hip hops most accomplished artist by the name of L.G. Wise. Gerod was being mentored and discipled by him along with a number of other hip-hop artists who traveled the country reaching those lost and suffering. I also remember seeing him perform in Lansing, Michigan at the Breslin Center packed out with over 15,000 people hanging on the edge of their seat as he performed and ministered to them. Even then, years ago, he had a hunger and passion to use his disadvantages to help others have an advantage and win in life.

I am so honored to see the great man that Gerod Sturgis has become. I could tell you all day of all of his accomplishments such as writing, producing and performing multiple albums, being the first African-American barber in our city, and also starting the first African-American owned barber college in our city that is now educating others to achieve their goals and dreams. All of that is wonderful but what's even greater is the fact that he is a Godly man, Godly husband, Godly father, and servant to his local church and his entire community.

Finally, when I think of Gerod I always remember the scripture in Jeremiah 1:5 that says, *"before I formed you in the belly I knew you, and before you came forth out of your mother's womb I sanctified you, and I ordained you to be a prophet to the nations."* He would always say, "That's my verse!" and this verse is a true picture of who Gerod Sturgis is. He's an overcomer, and I am confident that every person that reads this book will have the same vigor and faith to overcome all of the adversities of their lives. Regardless if you are faced with addiction, depression, oppression, fatherlessness, abuse, or anything that has made you believe that you can't win in life, allow Gerod's testimony of being "Lost, Now Found" to give you the strength that you need to tap the potential that God has placed on the inside of you.

~ Pastor Claude Bevier
Founder/ Senior Pastor
Restore World Church
Author of "The Blueprint, a Man's Journey to Self-Discovery"
Founder of "The Turn Challenge"

Forward from: Apostle Ivory L. Hopkins

G-Rod Sturgis is one of my Son's in the Gospel who has had a profound journey and insight how the power of God delivered him from addiction built his life to become a powerful testimony and ministry of the Kingdom.

In this book "Lost Now Found Freedom from Addiction", you will gain knowledge on how to operate in your full potential and prophetic destiny.

His was literally saved from death to destiny I had the pleasure of being his mentor and Apostle, his book is filled with practical teaching and biblical insight of the miracle working power of God's transformation of his life.

Apostle Ivory L. Hopkins (aka The General of Deliverance)

Overseer and founder of Pilgrims Ministry of Deliverance

East Coast Chancellor of Rapha Deliverance University

Introduction

Have you ever asked yourself what is my purpose in life? What If God never decided to choose me for his masterpiece? You ever find yourself spaced out talking to yourself? Like... 'Well my life sucks. I don't have this... I can't afford that... I'm always going through this... no one understands me... I don't even understand myself! Why was I born if I know one day I'm going to die? Why taste life if life's going to be taken away from me?' How about this? Have you ever felt like regardless of whatever you do it seems like you just can't get it right or your efforts just aren't good enough?

We all ask these questions. We all have experienced tough things in life. Sometimes we feel as though we are not good enough as an individual. Whether it's because of the negative influences and words of our parents, friends and family, classmates, teachers, peers or whoever. They say, sticks and stones may break my bones, but words may never hurt me. I kind of disagree with that statement! Words can break a family, a home, a church, a community, a state, a nation; which can affect a generation!

While reading this book, you might find that you yourself were in a similar situation that I've been in. You may have been through it, or maybe you're in it right now, but you're seeking wisdom on how to get out. Maybe you know someone who has these struggles that we're going to dig into. What I do know for sure is that if you're reading thus far YOU MADE IT!!! There's light at the end of the tunnel! One thing that I've learned was after the pain comes healing! After the rain comes the sun!

SECTION 1
LOST

Chapter One
Lost My Way

When it comes to knowing our purpose we all want to know what we're supposed to be doing, where *we*'re supposed to be doing it at, why we are to do it, when we're supposed to carry things out, and most of all, we want to know the answer to the age-old, most important question... WHO AM I? *We* were made in God's Image and after His likeness, according to Genesis 1:26. But there was another voice who crept in to speak to Adam and Eve to throw them off of their course, which caused them to lose their identity and made way for a curse to come upon the land. So many people are still suffering from that curse right now!

GOD gave Adam dominion to name things. He named all the animals and whatever name he gave, so be it; and it was. You must understand that according to Psalms 139:14, you are fearfully and wonderfully made; there isn't another you!!! When I think of fearfully it explains how careful and cautious God was in designing you. Imagine carrying a fragile expensive glass and afraid you might break it as you place it in a cupboard because of its value. Well God carefully fearfully made you special and unique he made you valuable! Wow when I heard that revelation it made me look at myself and God different. When he said you where wonderfully made, he made you in AWE. You no how people say I don't know what it is about you that I like that's that wonder in Psalms 139:14. A lot of people who don't know there purpose in life or know the father don't understand your "Wonder" You have been fearfully and wonderfully made God was afraid to mess up on you that's how important you are to him regardless of what you think. The enemy job is to have you thinking everything else about you so you can say the wrong thing and to get people to agree with you so you can forfeit your destiny and live a life that was never design for you to live or experience. He recognizes that death and life is in the power of the tongue. You have the ability to call those things that be not, as though they are! Meaning, if you think you're a nobody you will act like a nobody. If you don't think you're special, no one will treat you like you're special. If you don't think you could be a millionaire, chances are, you will never become a millionaire. Let's start naming animals like Adam did! Let's stand up and be who we were born to be and tap into your purpose! Mankind is still 'naming' destructive things today and getting upset at God when what we say manifests itself.

In my many years in ministry and counseling people, as I'm encouraging them to move forward to their potential of greatness in life, I've heard so many stories of devastating, painful experiences. One of these might be a hidden cry of your heart. You might be thinking, 'But you don't know my life! You don't know that I cry myself asleep at night! You don't know that I've been raped or molested! You don't know that I have AIDS! You don't know that I'm an orphan, my parents gave me up and I've been from home to home! You don't know that I never met my father and been raised by women with no father figure and have begun to question my identity! You don't know that I got pregnant at an early age, had an abortion and now I regret it. I can't sleep at night, awakening to a cry of a baby's voice that won't go away. You don't know that my husband beats me every night. Or that my boyfriend tries to kill me if I leave him. Maybe I'm in a marriage that's verbally abusive and very sheltered and wish I can leave, but don't want to hurt my children. You don't know that life had me down so much where I pray at night that I could just go to a secret island where I could be free. Or that I pray at night that God will take me in my sleep so I wouldn't have to deal with this pain. You don't know me!!!! The doctor tells me I have cancer with 3 months to live, you do not know me!!!

You're right, I don't know you! But I know someone who does! Trust me, that's the whole purpose of this book. Out of a million sperm cells, God hand-picked YOU!!! He knew every obstacle that you would face; he knew every battle, every scar, and every pain. I really want you to realize there are a million cells racing to that egg. The next time you think that you're not good enough, the next time you feel as though you don't have what it takes, I want you to think of that sperm racing, a billion sperm cells and how you fought your way through that race to get in that egg. God placed his DNA inside of you and put His mark on you. You are significant, you swam different, you maneuvered different, there was something in you that fought. Paul said, "*I fight the good fight of faith*." 1 Tim 6:12. From the beginning the enemy has been telling you that you're not going to make it, but you did! Don't stop now! Like the movie, Black Panther, when T'Challa's mother cried out during the battle, "Show him who you are!" something ignited in him and he begin to win. There's a winner inside of you. No matter how you feel don't let that dictate who you are!

There's a story about a man who walks into a grocery store and told the clerk good morning. The clerk was having a bad day and replied, "what's so good about this morning?" The gentleman then said, "try missing one." The moral was as long as there's breath in your body, you're blessed. We all go through life. I guarantee, if you heard some tragic stories of others, you would be like, 'man their life is rough, but man, what I'm going through is not as bad as that situation, so I'm grateful.' Why? Because regardless of the situation you're in, God's plan is for you to win! Jeremiah 29:11 says, "*For I know the thoughts that I think toward you, says the Lord, thoughts of peace and not of evil, to give you a future and a hope.*" See, God knows you and is thinking about you, so don't listen to that voice telling you that you're all alone. Instead think thoughts of peace, not of evil. So, if you think that God has any evil thoughts about you, then those thought patterns should be erased. John 3:17 says, "*For God sent not his Son into the world to condemn the world; but that the world through him might be saved.*" When I think of the word condemn, I think of property needing to be torn down. Something that was existing but needing to be demolished, not set or good for living; needs to be torn down. Does that sound like God's plan for you? No! He's a father that would build you up. Satan lives and thrives off of condemnation because he knows that that's the fuel that would leave *you* to self-infliction. He doesn't have to do anything but to put his thoughts in your head and you will do the rest.

The enemy always shows you an image, but it doesn't become life until you speak it. For example, if you would look in the mirror from after having a bad day and all you see is defeat, or you start seeing flaws because of how you see yourself in that situation, instead of How God created you and how he wired you, you will start looking and believing what the enemy said. Then you will begin to question yourself. That's the trick of the enemy to have you snared by your own words. Imagine coming home having a good day hearing positive words, confident looking in the mirror, and if Satan tries to show you images of defeat it has no weight because you're confident knowing who you are. There's life and death in the power of the tongue, then boom: it manifests. But remember what Jeremiah 29:11 says, *"I have thoughts of peace to give you that expected end."*

A lot of people fail in life because they're used to people saying, 'don't get your hopes up, don't expect that to happen.' But God is saying in Hebrews 11 to have the God kind of faith, to have your hope in Him that He will manifest what you're believing. Because when you put your trust and dependency on man, they will let you down because they have problems and situations just like you, with good intentions, but they're trying to figure life out as well. That's like asking the product, "Hey product, why were you made?" instead of asking the manufacture. So, no matter what, don't condemn yourself. Remember, God came to free you, not to bang you for all of your wrongs. He has no evil thoughts towards you. Now you know where those thoughts are coming from, they're fueled by satan. You've messed up, we all have. Sure, you've struggled, ran into hardships, been dealt a bad hand. Being lost is not a sensational feeling. It's a feeling of fear it's a feeling of abandonment, a feeling of isolation, it's a feeling of defeat. But being found, loved, appreciated, accepted and understood is such a beautiful place to be. Just think how you feel when you've lost something very valuable and nothing mattered until you found it. That's how it was with God he sent his only begotten Son to the world to save mankind to recover what was lost. Heaven stops in its tracks and rejoice when just one soul who is lost find God. That's how important you are to him. That's how much he cares for you that angels rejoice in the mist of salvation. His ultimate goal is for you to recover and discover everything that He placed inside of you!

Chapter Two
Dead on Arrival

Proverbs 14:12 *"There's a way that seems right to a man but in the end it leads to death."*

I was raced to the hospital by ambulance. "Code blue!" I heard them shout to one another as they documented the time of my death on October 31, 1999. I remember it just like it was yesterday.

It was October 30th around 8pm. I just got off of work and was heading to my Aunt's house, where I was staying at the time. As soon as I got there, I started changing my clothes and getting ready to meetup with a bunch of people to go out. Now, everybody started showing up to the house so when I hear a knock at my Aunt's door, I figured it was someone else getting ready to ride out with us. But when I opened up the door, to my surprise, it was my Mother (RIP). She drove all the way down to where I was at to reach me because she felt something wasn't right. If anyone ever really knew my Mom, she always "just knew" before something crazy was about to happen. She said, "son I'm begging you, do not go out tonight. Whatever money you have, give it to me." I'm like yeah right, so you can go shopping, and laughed it off. But the look she had on her face was like she knew I wasn't coming home. So, I'm thinking, ok, am I going to get robbed or shot? I told the fam to grab the guns.

So, we ended up partying at the house for a while. We had a crazy house party with lots of drugs and alcohol there. At the time my crew and family were headed to a Bad Boy concert. We had a couple of artists that were linking up on some business ventures with the label in New York City. The party was jumping so tough that we never even made it out there. We left the house party and we ended up cruising and hanging at different spots with my family (and friends that were like family). I was a drug dealer and I would buy just to take care of my family and myself, not to be the next Scarface or King of New York because I knew what came with the territory. I noticed that night everywhere I went people were being nice to me. I would go to different territories to try different products to see who had the best. So, I got a pass with one of my Big Homies who I was with. I got some cocaine off of this guy and he was like since this is your first time buying with us, I'm going to throw you an extra gram I was like bet; this is my lucky night! I received an ounce of weed I didn't have to pay the full amount for and almost a quarter of cocaine. Then, my friend bought me a case of Budweiser and a pint of Hennessey. It's not like they haven't seen me in a while, it's not like it's my birthday. They just did it for love. Which now I realize this was a trick of the enemy to kill me.

A week prior to all of this, a friend of my Mom came to me at my job just to deliver me a message that God told her concerning me. With the expression on her face all intense, she looked me right in my eyes and said, "Gerod, Jesus is calling your name. Don't ignore Him, answer. He wants you to come back home". I just said ok, and kind of blew her off.

That same night we went on to another party at a hotel. There was one guy who we didn't bring with us, and I felt bad because he always gets left behind and I'm like, let's go back and get him. The guys with me were like, "Nah we're late, we gone!" and made a joke behind it. Well, we started getting high at the club, made some stops, met up with some females, we bought them drinks and went about our way. We ended up back over our Aunt's house where I stayed at the time. We didn't want to ride dirty (as they say) and at this time it's about 5am, going into Halloween day. We smoked every ounce of weed, drunk every liquid within the bottle, and sniffed every bit of cocaine we saw.

I never slept at all that night. I pulled an all nighter because I had to work the next morning so I'm like hey, I might as well stay up. I started feeling really funny, so I got up to use the bathroom. I heard a loud bang. My friend who we left behind happened to be up and saw my face before I noticed him. He looked at me like he saw a ghost which made him to drop the dish in his hands in a panic and it shattered to pieces. All of a sudden, all of my strength completely left me, and I collapsed and fell to the floor. He was there to my aide and picked me up and carried me to the upstairs bathroom. When I looked in the mirror my eyes where blue, my face was turning pale, and my body was freezing cold. I even had a pimple that started oozing. I'm like man, what's happening to me?

He took me outside to the car, and the sky looked like it was judgment day: half black and the other half clear. My head was hanging out the window like a dog gasping for air because I couldn't breathe. He was getting ready to take me to a house that had a phone because there were no cellphones those days. We went over the house of the same guy who gave me the drugs to make the call. He turned around and gave me a bible and told me to read it. I looked at him and stuck it in my pocket. My friend who drove me over to his house is on the phone and I'm thinking he's calling the ambulance, but he called my parents. I was afraid because I grew up in a Christian home and I was ashamed of my parents seeing me like this. My parents immediately came over to where I was at and took me to their house and in the van ride over there, I kept yelling the name JESUS. Shouting JESUS have mercy on me, and I repeated his name over and over. When we got to my parents' home, they called the ambulance immediately. At the age of 19, right there in the living room, hands lifted, fighting for my life and the last breath I used was to praise God and yell his name. All the while, I see the tears rolling down my mother and father's face and I feel my life leaving my body.

The ambulance finally arrives to the house and they put me on the stretcher and get me inside the vehicle, check my pulse, and put the oxygen mask on. I heard them say in panic to one another, "He doesn't have a pulse." I heard those words and immediately rose up and said, "What do you mean I don't have a pulse?" Now there speeding with the sirens blazing and lights flashing, "we have a live one!" They ask me my name, I tell them Gerod Sturgis. They ask me my address, what day is it, how old I am, and I tell them. They *went* to draw blood from one arm and no blood. Tried to draw from my other main arm, and still couldn't draw any. Now they're poking me everywhere and checking my pulse again in amazement and confused, wondering how I'm still breathing, talking, and alive and so accurate with every question. The whole time I'm calling on Jesus I'm reading His Word that was tucked in my back pocket from one of the dealers placing it there.

I remember in my younger days I stopped believing in God. I said, "God if you're real then why did this happen, and why did that happen. I'm not gonna believe You until You come down here Yourself". That came back to my memory. When we arrived at the hospital and the paramedics were rushing me in, I saw one of my high school classmates who had become a nurse there. I was very athletic in High School, and she was one of the cheerleaders that placed snacks and decorated our locker for the games. I was shocked to see her, and she was just as shocked to see me. I asked her, "Heather, am I gonna make it?" Fighting the tears in her eyes she said, "Gerod, I heard the call and had to see with my own eyes. Truth be told there were three people who came in a couple hours before you and unfortunately, they didn't make it. Looking at everything, you're three times worse than them". That crushed all my hope, but I heard a voice say, "trust in Me, My *Word* is Life". I pulled the Bible out of my pocket and began to read it. Another nurse said, "That's your only hope reading that thing. Put him over with the rest of them."

I cried out and said, "God, I'm only 19, I can't die yet." When I opened the bible it went straight to Deuteronomy Chapter 28, the blessings and the curses, I read all the way up to Deuteronomy 30:19. "*I call Heaven and earth to witness against you this day that I have set before you life and death; blessings and curses,* therefore choose life, so that both you and your decedents may live". And I said, "God, if you save me, I promise with Your help I'll live for you, and share my testimony across the world." When I said that I heard the machine flat line. I had an outer body experience. God took me back from when I was a kid all the way up to the funeral. Everyone was mourning and crying and I'm telling them, "I'm here!" yet I'm seeing the spiritual battle take place for my soul. I said, "God, I'll serve you!" At the same time, I heard, "heart surgery in room 3". I'm like, "wait, I'm in room 3".

I heard the machine come to normal and I woke up. I'm seeing the machine about to enter and I'm like, am I tripping, what just happen? They all said we have no clue what and how. I said I know God healed me, I'm ready to leave. I jumped up off of the bed and immediately started trying to pull off all of the wires and monitors connected to me, but they stopped me and persisted that I wait so they can check and verify that my vitals were stable enough for me to leave. The police were there, and they had documented my death already. They said this is a miracle due to your body size, staying up 48 hours, and with the amount of drugs you took you should have died instantly. The police immediately just ripped up the report out of amaze and said, "promise me you will never do this again". I told them, "Oh, I promise this is something that I would never want to go through again in my life".

Chapter Three
Abuse

Romans 6:23 *"For the wages of sin is death, but the gift of God is eternal life in Christ Jesus our Lord."*

When you don't know the purpose of a thing, you could abuse a thing. If you don't know the purpose of chopsticks you can use them as drumsticks and misuse or abuse what it was created to do. I was just casually getting high. I was what they call a functioning addict. But don't you dare call me an addict, because in my eyes I serve addicts, but I never even knew that I was one. I looked at them as less than, and I judged them, until God put me in their shoes. Not all addicts enjoy where they are. They're basically screaming or what I call in one of my hit singles, "Crying Out". It starts as a casual drink, until they try to match the substance with their pain or with their trauma. (If you notice most addicts go through the same trauma or pain when they get high.) They talk about their problems, with a solution that one day they're going to quit. One day we're going to get help until someone overdose and it becomes more pain and torment, and they begin to lose their house, their kids, their job, to the point they have nothing. So, the real thing that they're facing is not chasing the next high, or that drug that gives them near death. Or even worse someone who rebels from their parents or someone going to a party for the first time gets high for the first time and gets laced and dies instantly. Or gets date raped from a drug not knowing what happened the next day, body found weeks later. Or someone so laced where they don't know who they are; lost their mind.

The real thing people face is being lost. I had one of the coolest friends, popular in school, ladies' man, everyone wanted to be like him and hang around him. One drug changed his life. He went on a mental trip and lost it all, like PTSD, he just flips out and literally became mentally ill. People are lost. They're lost because of abandonment. Abandonment is the gateway to addiction, whether its sexual or whether it's love as a whole. At the end of the day, it's a love deficiency. Without it, people will go back into default mode. With so many broken homes, so many Fathers incarcerated, women abused, children stripped from homes, street family known as Gangs. All are looking for one thing with a closed mouth, the answer to the question, WHO AM I? Unable to get fed because of anger and rejection, built walls of malice and rage. Disappointments and let downs, so they look for an escape which is easier to find in a drug because its instant, rather than going to the gym, playing basketball, etc. People are afraid of outlets like that because they've become a custom to rejection, living in a busy society where there's not enough time so abuse becomes amplified upon the playing fields of a tormented mind. And its reality doesn't surface until it becomes you, or someone close to you. Now its preparation for a funeral. Death of a loved one. But the death did not take place with the drug abuse.

Adam was so full of life that he had to learn how to die. When you disconnect a water hose from a faucet there's still water trickling down the hose but, eventually the water runs out. Abuse is birthed out of separation. That's why in the beginning of the Bible in the book of Genesis when God created the heavens and the earth and every creeping thing, He said it was good and He put seed within everything He created. And He created everything after its own kind but when He made man, He created Him after His kind. In the God class in His image and His likeness and place His seed within man to reproduce to be fruitful, multiply, subdue, take dominion because that's what He did in the beginning. He then realized an issue with mankind after He gave the mandate. Notice in scripture He said everything was good but when He got to man, He said it's not good that man be alone all one. So He created a help meet. He created accountability. This world is wired on relationships! When mankind is separated or all one in any area of his life mentally, physically, or socially abuse is inevitable.

Again, in Genesis when the man was separated from the woman the serpent tricked Eve into eating the fruit and she gave it to her husband, and he ate. Then God said, "Adam, where are you?" (Separation). God is omnipotent, God is all knowing. He wasn't speaking of geographical location he was speaking from a Spiritual aspect, as we would do to one another. To our children family or friends like, "Where are you? or What were you thinking?" You know how it is when you put your trust in someone and they do something unbelievable to the point where you can't believe it, so you ask that question "Have you lost your mind?" Your saying, where are you? Lol! Notice in the state of being lost you tend to abuse or hurt not just yourself but others. Notice once you're in this state of mind you begin to shift blame! Adam blamed the woman, the woman blamed Satan. Who are you blaming? Gen 3:12 The man said, *"The woman you put here with me she gave me some fruit from the tree and I ate it."* You can be in a bad situation so long until it looks good. You can convivence yourself that nothing is wrong with you. Everyone can see the changes, but you're so comfortable in you mess that you don't recognize it. That's how I was. I didn't realize I was getting thinner, irritable, and angry. Slowly loosing everything. Hurting the very ones that love me. We all heard the saying hurting people hurt people.

Poem
Testimony

October 31st, I wasn't even thinking of a hearse

Headed back to the dirt over a family-line curse

Let me get deeper; I was faced to face with the reaper

I ate the wrong fruit, thinking life will get sweeter

Had it all planned: me and the fam, a couple of grams, on my way to Del state homecoming ready to jam

In the meanwhile, we was getting nice, I had the blunts rolled tight, had my head piece right

Not thinking that the enemy comes like a thief in the night

Had a 5th of Henny, drugs we had plenty. Stage like this you can tell it wasn't friendly

Sold a couple of sacs, had to get my money back. Alright now, let's get this car back on track

Let's head north! Instead we made a stop at the courts. We stopped to this girl house and the time wasn't short

Right there was another chronic break, another pop to take, another Hennessy bottle to shake

It seemed kind of weird. How did I get here? Like ghost town, whoa now, everyone disappeared

I started to think about the end times, feeling left behind. Jesus must of came back while I was out of line

Mind going crazy, head all hazy, losing my breath, close to death.

God please can you save me?

He's a God of a second, third and fifty chances

That's why I give him Praise in every circumstance

SECTION 1 DISCUSSION QUESTIONS

1. Who are you?

   _____
   _____
   _____
   _____
   _____

2. What roadblocks are stopping you from becoming the real you deep inside?

   _____
   _____
   _____
   _____
   _____

3. What was the crossroad in your life that set you at your final decision to change?

   _____
   _____
   _____
   _____
   _____

4. What do you do when you realize you are abusing yourself?

   _____
   _____
   _____
   _____
   _____

SECTION 2
RELATIONSHIPS

Chapter Four
Hiding

When we mess up, we usually have a tendency of hiding. Adam hid because he messed up. When I messed up, I hid from all those who would've held me accountable. I wouldn't answer my phone, I'd go missing for days, I would crawl in a so-called dark place and isolate myself. My pastor would always say, "Isolation equals amputation. You begin to cut off the very help you are in need of". Notice when your all alone you hear all types of voices and you begin to take action, or you sink into a deeper hole, depending on how emotional you feel in the state you're in. Some will hear condemnation and will remain or get worse, while others may hear their support team or accountability system telling them, I believe in you, this is not who you are! Depending on whose voice you hear the most will determine how you see yourself. That's why it is very important to hear the voice of God.

John 10:27-28 *"My sheep hear my voice, and I know them, and they follow me: And I give unto them eternal life; and they shall never perish, neither shall any man pluck them out of my hand."*

Adam immediately tried to cover himself because he saw himself different, he saw himself naked, and began to sew fig trees for him and his wife. Again, he knew enough to cover his wife after the fall, but not know enough to cover her during the call. God says, 'who told you that you were naked?' Notice before the fall they *were* naked and not ashamed because they were in His presence and full of his Glory being led and controlled by Him. It wasn't until they separated themselves and ate the bait of Satan that they realized they were naked. Today God is still asking you and I, 'Who told you that you were naked? Who told you that you were sick? Who told you that you were poor? Who told you that you would never amount to anything? Who told you that you were too fat, too skinny, that your skin disqualifies you, that your speech sounds off? Who told you that you're a mistake, that you're going to be just like your mother, just like your father?" God made you in His image and in His likeness. Remember that!

Numbers 23:19 *"God is not a man, that he should lie; neither the son of man, that he should repent: hath he said, and shall he not do it? or hath he spoken, and shall he not make it good?"*

One thing you must understand is that the real enemy knows how to trap the "inner me". It's the voice you hear that tells you not to obey the Holy Spirit. Once you receive salvation if you're not born again you will feel an unction and tug or something saying to you, "don't go there, don't do that, don't take that, don't say that, don't look at that, don't take that number, etc." Without accepting the Lord Jesus Christ as my personal savior, I was unable to understand or hear his voice clearly and I decided to take a different route, ignoring the red flags. It's very easy to be swayed by other voices. The bible states that the sheep hears my voice and the voice of a stranger he will not follow. It's very easy to hide. Halloween isn't the only time people hide behind a costume. There may be people you look up to or maybe family members or key elite Entertainers or Athletes that's hiding. There's nothing hidden that wouldn't be made manifest. A person who haven't tapped into God's plan and purpose for their life, who gives true identity will always hide behind a costume.

Chapter Five
Accountability

Proverbs 27:17 *"As Iron sharpens iron, so one person sharpens another"*

I never assume that everyone has a relationship with God but, this is what worked for me, so I want to offer you the formula that I used. If you decide to or not, this is what worked for me. Those who are sick and tired and tried everything possible... I'd like to take this time out right here, right now, and offer you salvation. Right now? Yes, right now! Who says that you have to wait until everything is perfect? If you're sick you would need medicine right now, not when your healed. If you're hungry you need food right now, not when you're full. If you see your boat is sinking why wait until your drowning to be rescued. I heard a familiar story anonymous about someone who was drowning, and they were in need of rescue and God sent them a helicopter, but they refused because they were expecting God to save them. Then God sent them a boat for help, and they refused, and they said no, I'm waiting on God to rescue me. I'm gonna add this, there was a guy jet skiing and he too was lost asked the other gentlemen for direction. The gentlemen gave him direction and the guy on the jet ski turned around and said kindly begging, 'please sir get on the back of my jet ski it's starting to be dark and you're in the middle of nowhere. You gave me direction, in return please let me get you back to safety!' The guy in return said it's fine, God's gonna save me. Well the gentlemen end up not making it. He went to Heaven and he asked God, "God, why didn't You rescue me?" God said, "when I sent you the helicopter, that was me trying to rescue you. When I sent you to that boat that was me trying to rescue you. Lastly when I sent you the jet ski was my final offer and because it was not what you expected, you refused. Isn't it funny how we can have good advice or can help others but when we need the help or advice we know how; we just choose not to? Well again, that's the enemy using the inner me to trap you within your thoughts. I'd like for you to repeat after me:

Prayer of Salvation

Dear God, I am humbly calling out to You. I'm tired of doing things my way to get my results. I realize that you are the Way and I want to do things Your way so I can get Your results. I invite You into my life to be my Lord and Savior. Fill the emptiness in me with Your Holy Spirit and make me whole. Lord help me trust You, help me love You, help me to live for You. I believe that Jesus died on the Cross for our sins and rose on the third day and is now seated at the right hand of God. I believe with my heart and confess with my mouth, for He made Him who knew no sin to be sin for us for me that I may become the righteousness of God in Jesus' name, Amen!

WELCOME TO THE KINGDOM!!!!

John 3:16, *"For God so loved the world that He gave His only begotten Son, that whosoever believes in Him shall not perish, but have everlasting life."*

Chapter Six

Relationships

Almost everything in life, good or bad, is connected to relationships! This is a huge aspect in life that I believe we've missed tremendously. Now it's very important that you don't read this chapter too fast because this chapter is what changed my life and could determine the altitude of yours as well. I've noticed in the book of Genesis Chapter 1, when God created everything, He created it in seed form. Once He did that, He told man, 'now you have dominion over every seed-bearing fruit and animal,' and with that He made the seed within itself. Mankind is the seed of God, that's why He said, "*Let Us make man in Our Own Image and Our Own likeness*". First thing He did was released the Blessing!! Genesis 1:28 says, "*And God blessed them, and God said unto them, Be fruitful, and multiply, and replenish the earth, and subdue it: and have dominion over the fish of the sea, and over the fowl of the air, and over every living thing that moveth upon the earth.*" So the Blessing of reproduction was on the man Adam's life; his responsibility was so powerful and heavy that he had to stay connected and accountable with the Father. After He released the blessing, He released the commandment. The same way He called to the light, "Let there Be light," He said Be fruitful. In other words, LIGHT BE>>> FRUIT BE!!!!! Not only to multiply it but replenish it over and over. When He realized man was alone God gave the mandate but there was no accountability for the man, so when He created the woman, He said this is very Good! Now He can see the system was complete.

I was praying one day, and God said, "Son I've wired this world based upon relationships and multiplications. Family is a form of relationships where you have companionship and friendship. The issue is many people who don't really understand their value, or their worth don't fully get the clear picture of who they really are, so they connect with like-minded people who relate to their pain instead of their passion. You can't even have a job without having a relationship with the boss, manager or employee. Now determining upon your character and what's in your heart will be the factor upon those relationships; good or bad. I feel every day we are faced with the opportunity of what type of fruit we're going to eat or what type of relationship we're going to benefit from good or bad.

Ask yourself what type of relationships you have. Now I'm not talking about the minor things that take place in a relationship that everyday people experience like disagreements, arguments, light space then your right back being best friends. I'm speaking of toxic relationships that pull you down. You may be celebrating recovery being clean for 5 days which may be a big step, or clean for 3 years. Rather than that person celebrating with you they're jealous because it's taking them longer because they don't know how to change their environment. Therefore, they can't change because of the people that are in their environment may seem to be unable to break the mold and wondering how you did it. Now they're looking at you thinking, 'oh you think you're better than everyone else'. If you don't change your environment, then soon the environment will change you.

I saw it so often in the past when I was blind of the environment I was in, and I see it so many times in celebrating recovery. When you've got to go to the same city you messed up in; the same house, the same job, the same people; before you know it, it's the same problem. For me, it wasn't until I was held accountable and taught the Word of God where I realized that, 'hey, I have a purpose in life, the Kingdom of God lives in me and I have the power to change my surroundings,' but it takes work. I had to fight the good fight of faith until I was strong enough to be able to face my giants and win in life. I decided to move to a different city to break away from people, even my family and friends. I took a pay cut because my freedom meant more than everything just so I can know the Father! I could've done it where I was maybe, but I don't like cycles and I found myself repeating too many cycles and I didn't want to become a statistic or another number!

I remember like it was yesterday; it was May 2006 and my divorce had just been finalized. I was staying in a boarding home and working at a Rent-A-Center. During this time, I was dealing with lots of trauma. I just had a divorce because I found out the baby girl that I loved and raised for 4 years, who had my name wasn't my child. Right after that I lost my grandmother who I've always been close with my whole life. I immediately went into default mode. Now previous to all of this, I was a gospel rapper who gave my life to the Lord. I was connected and accountable. I had a strong system but when that trauma took place my friends who weren't connected to God begin to take me out to get my mind off things, and instead of running to God I ran away from Him. So, they begin to feed me with words and take me to the strip club and set me up with females to get revenge. I began to drink then smoke until I found myself back to the state that I promised God that I would never go back to. I then start selling drugs again. One day we are at the strip club and one of my homeboys tells the stripper as we buy her a drink, "you know he's a gospel rapper?" I'm like OMG not here my guy! So, they have a full convo and he slips her my CD and she chuckled and said thank you I will give this to my son. A couple weeks later I found myself bored one night, alone, looking for companionship, even if it was temporary, so I went to the strip club that my friend took me to. I asked for the stripper who was there that night and to my surprise they said she no longer worked there, and I'm like "wow what happened, does she work at another location?" She said, "Oh no dear. This is an unbelievable story I got to share it with you. A gentleman gave her some gospel rap CD and she only danced to get money for her son because he stayed in trouble and she was praying that someone could get through to him. He listened to the CD and his life was changed so he began to change all the way and she just quit." I'm frozen at this moment as she said, "Isn't that like unbelievable?" and I'm like "yeah it sure is!" So, I put my hoody on and walked away totally embarrassed and confused to the point like, "ok God, that was a good one lol".

Another time I was selling weed and no one knew my real name at the area I was in so I changed my name and used a nickname I made up from a movie I saw. I had a street code. This girl was looking for some weed. I was staying with my cousin and she asked my cousin if she knew anyone and she was like yea I do I'll send him over. Now at the time I brought some to her and it was at night and I kept a hoody on and always wore dark clothes. We made the exchange and she was like, "wait don't I know you?" I said, "absolutely not, I'm not from around here, I'm just visiting." She asked me, "Are you a rapper?" I told her no, then she said, "wow, you look just like this dude I listen to. I have his CD" and she showed me the cover and I said, "wow, he does favor me. Well they say everyone has a twin". Now I'm like, 'ok God what are you doing here!! I'm done, can you let me just go through like everyone else? Can I just be a victim for once?! Why are you harassing me?' I told my cousin what happened. She just laughed and said you're marked you don't belong out here no more! I said it's not fair, but ok! I went to my old church and I was looked at like I was a nobody. The same churched that I tithed at, sang at, ministered at, etc; I wasn't welcomed home like the prodigal son. I felt what a sinner would feel if they walked in the doors and it turned me off. After that I just went deeper.

I went to another area to set up shop; stayed over my homeboys' crib and I used an alias name when I sold drugs. One day there was a guy who was short on money and he said I have a CD player I can give you just follow me. Totally different city now, and a different time. So, I go in, and he plays this CD. "What's this?" I asked. He says, "It's a song I made up." And I said, "ok let me here it really quick." He presses play, as I bag up my product and as he does, I just sink! He's dancing and rapping my whole song! I asked him, "You wrote this?" He says yes. And I then rapped the second verse and he looked all surprised and said, "Woah!"

I said, "Man this is me! This is my album!" He cried out, "NO WAY! Man, I'm sorry, I apologize. I rap this every time I get high and when I'm going through it ministers to me." I said, "Nah I apologize. Keep the CD player." I walked out, threw my hoodie up, and had a long talk with God. I realized that no matter where I was, I couldn't run from the love of God. How He reminded me, "You can't run from what I called you to do". Did I stop then, and ignore God again? Don't we all? You know how many times he calls us to do a certain thing for Him and we feel as though we're not capable or equipped to do so, or maybe we filed underqualified or may not fit the package that He wants delivered out. Who are we to judge that? Like it's said in Jeremiah 15:5-6 *"Before I formed thee in the belly, I knew thee; and before thou camest forth out of the womb I sanctified thee, and I ordained thee a prophet unto the nations. Then said I, Ah, Lord God! behold, I cannot speak: for I am a child."*

Notice how God ordained and called him, and the very next verse he began to look at his inabilities. So, I didn't stop even though it was loud and clear. I was getting off of work one day and this was a city known for making money off of little. I had a little package on me worth $120 at this time I was serving crack to the guy who had the CD player and to my next delivery was my older cousin for the sake of this book, I'll say his name is Tommy and Tommy was, let's say, a plumber. I admired him for being a "plumber". He was at all our gatherings and social events and there was a time I wanted what he had. As I got older, I would see him every now and then and we would small talk and I then got a family of my own and wasn't around as much. So back to the call, I received a call from one of my home girls from Jersey. She was like you want to make a couple dollars. I got a customer you can serve I'll tell him you on the way. So, I'm like, "shoot me the address". It's a dark road, it's night, the house is dark. I'm like, woah is this a setup? I have no weapon, battery low, I don't know about this one. I didn't get his name, only info was to bring it to him an easy swap.

When he finally came and turned the light on, which was dim, I kept my hoodie on for this one and I had shades on as a disguise. I exchanged I served him he gave me the money and the voice pierced me as he said wait. As he tested it, he said, "yea, I want to deal with you for now on." He grabbed my hand and said, "What's your name son?" I yelled, "Don't touch me!" aggressively and snatched my hand back in shame. I said, "It's Bishop and I'm only in for the night." He then showed me more money and said, "If you have more can I call you personally and I said, "I don't have no more for you!" and I ran out and sat in my car and cried. I can't believe I served crack to my own cousin. It may not mean anything to some people because I know some people that serve their uncles, aunts and even worse, their Mothers. I don't have that type of heart the love of money is the root to all evil. That was it for ME!

I then stopped selling, but I kept partying. This one night I had a female upstairs and it was getting late, but I told her, "listen I just want to chill tonight." So, I'm drinking and smoking and start channel surfing and I see this guy on TV named MYLES Munroe. He says the most profound thing I ever heard in my life! He said, "If you put water in a freezer in an ice tray what happens? It becomes ice! If you put that same water in a glass or a pitcher it becomes water. But if you dump that water into a saucepan or a pot and turn the heat real high and put it on a stove then what happens it becomes steam! The same substance, but it really only changes its environment!" WOW! That changed my life! I immediately got high and kicked everyone out of my house and began to pray. My environment wasn't conducive enough for me to grow, so I had to change it. I had too many wrong people in my life, where I then became the negative influencer. Take a look at the 5 closest people that you're connected to. You can judge your future by who you're connected to. Never desire to trade places with someone who has no substance or direction of achieving what you desire! It wasn't until I surrendered unto God and totally realized and accepted that my life is not my own. I've been bought with a price and I belong to God. Whatever I'm here to do for God I accepted, and my goal is to help others to realize their potential and what God has for them that's been covered up by defeat!

Chapter Seven
The Wake-Up Call

Sometimes we can forget that God will put people in our path momentarily using them so He can work through to you. I had what looked like the perfect life. Married with children, attending church, doing sports with my kids, going shopping, having fun with my friends, full time management job at Rent-A-Center making 65k a year plus bonuses. Then one day my marriage took a crap and I still tried to work it out for the sake of God and my children. But when there was cheating involved, on top of lies and more drama added to the fire, the type of guy I was it would be best for me to leave. I knew my kids would been my hardest, toughest battle. They love me with everything because I gave them all my love. I still till this day remember when my 4-year-old daughter ran out the house and chased my car down screaming daddy. That was the most ripping thing I've ever experienced. My son was a baby and it was very hard. Every night I cried and try to drown my pain with some type of substance or female to try to fill a void only God could fill.

I started to drink again. I was at bars night after night after I promised myself that I would never return there. I said this in my song "Dope", 'People don't wake up and say, I think I want to be an addict today'. No, something had to happen, something traumatic, to cause them to really go backwards in most not all cases. I lost everything and felt less than a man. Then every negative word of failure I heard in my life I started to believe because I was living in my car showing up to work drunk. I was too embarrassed to go to family and friends, so I took this journey alone and went back to drugs.

My boss at Rent-A-Center seen me go backwards and everyone on the job started complaining to him. I overheard a coworker tell him, "You need to fire him! He drinks on the job, smokes, uses cocaine, speeding, short with the customers! He's not the same!" My boss would always take up for me though. I got into an accident with the work truck and he took up for me. He would come to work and see me asleep in front of the door, splash water on me and say go wash up in the back. He believed in me and didn't judge me when I was at my lowest when I didn't know what to do. Me as a devoted Christian now, I see how important that is because there would be Christians who knew me and wouldn't even speak because of the situation, not knowing the full story and seeing me go backwards, and just not showing the love of Christ. That did something to me! It pushed me away from church for a long time. That's why now I show love and empathy on everyone because I don't forget nothing! That man opened up his home to me. He was married with children and he gave me his private suite until I got on my feet. He said I refuse to allow all this potential in you go to waste. He knew I loved music because that's all I did, and he pushed me. He played my music in the store at Rent-A-Center and people would ask, 'who is that?' and he would say, 'that's young Mc Hammer' our little joke. He would always tell people, 'he's going places.' That's all I needed was someone to be there in my lowest.

Let's back it up to the night before he took me in, I was staying with a friend who also worked with me. We would party together at times and I had my last bag of cocaine. I had my 1 year old with me and I had drugs already in my system and was drinking a little and I was high. I held my son in my arms, and he gave me a look that ricocheted through my soul and it seemed like I heard his voice scream through his eyes saying, "Dad stop please, I need you! Don't do this to yourself. At least stop for me! I can't be Fatherless! I need my Father!" Mind you, he can't talk yet. I'm giving him a bottle, but his eyes said it all. That was it for me. I was done that night. I told his mom you need to come and get him. I went to sleep afraid I was going to die because of the amount of drugs I had taken and slept in front of the store around 5:30am.

That's when my boss saw me, he splashed water on my face and said to go in the back wash up and get myself together. The crazy thing is, I was never like this. I just dabbled here and there and next thing you know it got out of hand. But my manager and my son changed my life! I then left my job and moved to Michigan. I built up enough courage to connect with a rapper I knew. He was a minister and said, "you need to come down and ill help you". I knew that if I had a problem in Delaware, I would have a problem in Michigan, because my pastor would tell me wherever you are mentality you are physically the only difference is are you willing to change. I was willing! Sometimes you need to change your environment though and connect yourself with the right people. As I said in my previous chapter this world is wired for you to be accountable to someone a good relationship, or partner, or leader, or spouse, or friend, or Pastor who will tell you the truth help you elevate, show you your flaws and lead you in to the right direction! Had I not had that, this book would not have been written so you can receive the tools to build yourself into that great man, or that great woman that God created and called you to be. Deep inside you hear the voice of greatness to see yourself better than where you are right now. I hear you saying, "If I just had that push, or direction, or the Next step". Trust me I've been there, and the answer is accountability.

SECTION 2 DISCUSSION QUESTIONS

1. Have you ever hid yourself from people who loved you? If so, why?

   _____
   _____
   _____
   _____
   _____

2. How important is it to be accountable to someone? Explain

   _____
   _____
   _____
   _____
   _____

3. How did past relationships affect your life?

   _____
   _____
   _____
   _____
   _____

4. What was your wakeup call?

   _____
   _____
   _____
   _____
   _____

SECTION 3
MY ROAD TO DISCOVERY

Chapter Eight
Knowing the Father

I realized the whole time I was dodging accountability. I was dodging the Love of God. It's hard to Love if you don't have Love capacity. I grew up in a home where Love wasn't addressed verbally or physically. We just knew we loved each other because of certain boundaries that were set, or just the presence of all of us being in the room. Communication wasn't a big thing. I would walk in and walk out at times, we were not a hugging, emotional type of family. We expressed our love differently. So, it was challenging and hard for me to receive God's love because I didn't know what that looked like. I grew up thinking God was the person in the sky ready to bang you every time you do something wrong, not thinking or realizing that He is a Father. Like any Father loves their children. I didn't know Him. So, every female I came across I would hurt them and damage their feelings. I wasn't affectionate because I was taught that that was a sign of weakness. I wasn't able to give anything I didn't have, and I was tired of crushing everything that came my way. I had to receive the Love of God knowing that even in my mess, He still loves me.

Mark 12:30-31 *"Love the Lord your God with all your heart and with all your soul and with all your mind and with all your strength.' The second is this: 'Love your neighbor as yourself.' There is no commandment greater than these."*

This was very tough for me, especially knowing that faith worketh by Love. So, if Love wasn't in order then there would be no way my faith would work; no matter how much or what I believe. How can you love someone else genuinely if you don't love yourself? And how can you love yourself if you truly don't love or know the Father! Because God is love! I can say, "Oh, I love myself", but if I'm inflicting pain upon myself in a disguise of being hurt by someone, or I turned within and became isolated. I turned inwardly then guessed that I don't love me no matter what I may say, my actions aren't lining up. I'm not fooling anyone other than myself. That's how you have so many people addicted to things because they haven't locked in and got addicted to God's Love. If you Love God and He pours His love out to you, you wouldn't do certain things. Because I Love my wife no matter the temptation, I will never cheat on her because I love God, I Love myself, and I love my wife! I now channel everything through that formula: How would God feel? Am I representing God properly? Am I willing to lose my connection I have with Him after He delivered me, set me free, blessed me? Am I willing to put that on the line? Do I love myself? I avoid all pain if I have to, so I wouldn't want to self-inflict because I love freedom and stress-free living. I don't want to have to continue to fight harder than what I have to: I love me. And I love others! I don't enjoy or want to see anyone else suffer or hurt. So that's the formula I use for every situation. Knowing the Father is everything. In the beginning was the Word and the Word was with God, and the Word was God. We live life backwards. We chase destiny trying to find ourselves realizing that in finding ourselves we're lonely. Then we look for relationships because we're really searching for intimacy or companionship in any form, not knowing we're missing the void of an intimate Father who created us. So, we're not satisfied with the destiny or the path we chose because we don't like the person it made us become, or we're not experiencing the love or Joy.

My pastor, Claude Bevier, wrote a book that I will be referencing a lot called The Blueprint, and I find it as though it is the blueprint to life. He said a profound statement that I believe everyone should follow. Know God, Know yourself, Know your assignment. The formula he uses is Intimacy* Identity* Destiny. Ask yourself this: How can you know yourself without knowing the one who created you? Even more How can you know your assignment if you don't know who you are? Joyce Meyer once said, "You can climb the ladder of success and realize you're on the wrong roof". It would be a shame to do all that work, waste all that time chasing your destiny, losing yourself, not knowing the Father who can tell you in seconds who you are, what you're supposed to be doing, where you're supposed to go, and who you're supposed to link with. Instead we go thinking we know what's best and run into roadblocks and find ourselves in the ditches of life.

Chapter Nine
GPS – Gaining Personal Success

Psalms 37:23 "*The Steps of a good man are ordered by the Lord and He delighteth in his way*"

I know you're wondering about the GPS system. In planning any trip or place that you have never been you first have to do what I call GPS. Before putting in the destination or before the destination begins to start the GPS will talk, depending on what type you have. It will say now locating. Or it will ask you to put in your location. You can never go to your destination without first recognizing your location. You must be true to yourself. I notice a lot of people are anxious to get to a place without locating where they are first. Often times you may have been to that place before, not thinking you need direction. There's a route that I take every time we go out of town to our favorite restaurant and my wife always asks me to put the GPS on. I usually tell her that I don't need it because I know where I'm going. Now the route I normally have taken is out, and I am not familiar with the other surrounding roads, so I had to put the GPS on. I realized it doesn't matter how much you know or what you've experienced, there will be some valleys in life, some hiccups and roadblocks that you never planned. In life you will experience detours.

Like right now, were in the middle of a pandemic and my wife and I had to draw out new plans due to the coronavirus. I had to close my business down, my wife had to quit her job abruptly because they shut down all schools and we had no childcare, the states are on an emergency lockdown quarantine, only essential business like gas stations, grocery stores, are open; to name a few. Who would ever guess that churches wouldn't be able to fellowship that the first time ever in our history we can't celebrate Easter

(Resurrection Sunday), or Christmas together with family and friends? Only in the confounds of our home. That's a shock, a curve ball when the world has to shut down. Not just a country, you're talking the whole world! So, we have to put in a different location. I just can't operate the way I would normally operate I need direction!!! The world needs direction. Are you ready to go to that place? I see plenty of people get elevated to a place, but they never dealt with their character and lost it all. My Pastor would always tell me your altitude is determined by your attitude. In Genesis Chapter 3 when God asked Adam, "Where are you?" He wasn't asking again for a geographical location. He was basically saying, 'Adam you need to locate yourself because you separated yourself from the very life source.'

The bible says he was afraid, and he hid himself. When you hide you cover!! What are you covering up because you separated yourself? What type of relationship are you in because you hid for cover? Often times we live our life based upon someone's expectation of who we ought to be, not even understanding and realizing who God created you to be. Why did you go to football tryouts? Well, my father wanted me to play. Why did you got to college to be a doctor? Well, my mother wanted me to. There's nothing wrong with education, you will find out later that I'm all for it, 100 percent. What I'm saying is that you could get into a bad relationship, even being at the wrong place at the wrong time or trying a drug for the first time and ruin who you are by trying to fit a mold that wasn't designed for you. The bible says, "you are fearfully and wonderfully made!"

When you decide to live life based upon what others feel and think or looking at someone else's lifestyle and wanting what they have you are committing what I call emotional spiritual suicide. You are saying to God, "I don't appreciate the way you created me! I'm not happy with the life that I have. Why did you create me to live with this family and to be in this city and to suffer with this situation? Why, why, why, why? I want a refund." Your basically committing emotional spiritual suicide. That has nothing to do with God, but everything to do with you. Life is choice driven. You can never run away from you no matter how fast you are, wherever you are; you are!! Wherever you are physically is a product of where you're mentally. You can say, 'that's it I'm leaving New Jersey and moving to Florida'. Guess what if you are busted up in New Jersey all you're going to do is take your busted-up self to Florida until you locate yourself and seek freedom. You will remain a slave to bondage of your own pain.

Acts 16:25-30 *"About midnight Paul and Silas were praying and singing hymns to God, and the other prisoners were listening to them. Suddenly there was such a violent earthquake that the foundations of the prison were shaken. At once all the prison doors flew open, and everyone's chains came loose. The jailer woke up, and when he saw the prison doors open, he drew his sword and was about to kill himself because he thought the prisoners had escaped. But Paul shouted, 'Don't harm yourself! We are all here!' The jailer called for lights, rushed in and fell trembling before Paul and Silas. He then brought them out and asked, 'Sirs, what must I do to be saved?'"*

Notice you can't free no one else unless you're free yourself. Paul and Silas once freed, had the ability to free others. Often times we try to free people while were still locked down in chains. It wasn't until I became free from drugs and alcohol and a certain lifestyle that I was able to go back and free others. Knowing Who God is so He can then tell you who you are and have confidence in Him who gives you confidence!

Psalm 139:14 *"I praise you because I am fearfully and wonderfully made; your works are wonderful; I know that full well."*

Chapter Ten
Knowing Who I Am

Genesis 1:2 *"In the beginning God created the heaven and the earth. And the earth was without form, and void; and darkness was upon the face of the deep. And the Spirit of God moved upon the face of the waters."*

Knowing the purpose of a thing and assuming the purpose of a thing are two totally different things. Living life based upon certainty has a different effect than living an unsure life. A great question to ask yourself is; Who am I? That's the first step! My destination is based upon the makeup of who I am. It's impossible to know where you are going if you don't know where you are. It's what we call the GPS system. When I say, "know where you are at", I'm referring to who you presently are. I'm not talking about your habits, talents and ideas that's your makeup that allows others to see you. Ex. "Oh, that's a painter I've seen his work. She's a baker, I tasted her cheesecake. He's an awesome actor. He's a great singer." Your makeup is an outer image that identifies you with society. That's why you can do these things and still be unhappy. You hear a lot of "successful" people commit suicide who are millionaires, business owners, actors, singers, etc. because they left the stage or their platform to realize their emptiness. Because they're still on a soul search trying to figure out who they are. So, what is it? What makes you, you? Who is the real you? A person can be familiar with you but not really know the real you. Your family, your bloodline, your Father, Mother, brother, sister, etc. who grown up with you are familiar to the things you like, the things you admire, the things that trigger you, the things that shut you down. They even may believe that they know exactly what it is that makes you happy. But only the manufacture would truly know why every bolt, every screw, every washer is placed within the packaging of the product. And only the manufacturer provides the correct instructions on how to not only put the product together, but also how to operate that product. While growing up, you may have heard words spoken over you and to you that doesn't agree with your inner man. Harmful words like, "I hate you, your stupid, you will never amount to anything, you're just like your father, I wish I never had you." Believe it or not, you may not know, but those words do more damage than a fist to a face. Satan's number one trick is to confuse you to the point where you feel as though you were a mistake on this earth so you will abort your purpose and won't live out why God put you here. Like verse 2 in Genesis 1, *"darkness was upon the face of the earth"*. Sometimes we're going to feel like we've been misused mistreated, done wrong by parents, by our boss, our co-workers, family, friends, and loved ones. I mean, name just drug threw to the ground totally walked on. Well we were made from the ground. Just like the ground is walked on, water turns to mud, trash is thrown on there, but the ground is also where seeds are planted. Perception is everything!

That's when we must realize that we have the breath of life inside of us made form the Image of God. The first key of knowing who you are is first knowing who God is. Until you have a true relationship based on who God is you will never know who you are. I know you're probably saying well, I've got dreams, goals, talents and hobbies that I'm good at. Trust me I've done it all, you will find yourself always back to square one, asking yourself, "why can't I advance?", or "why this is always happening to me why everyone else around me is living a good life, and mine is mediocre?" Trust me, shortcuts don't always work. Always read the instructions because it may work fine for a while but somewhere down the line it will break down due to a missing piece. You must understand the mind of the manufacture in order to understand the product. Who you are has everything to do with who He is. I'm going to keep it real with you. I did not understand the bible. It was confusing. It was hard. It was frustrating. I began to get upset because I wasn't receiving what I wanted, and I couldn't do what I wanted to do. Even though I knew there was greater, I just couldn't see it. I got upset, shut down and got in my feelings. Then God gave me a revelation saying, "The way *you* feel is exactly how your wife feels. She doesn't understand you. She is frustrated, and she knows that you have more to offer, but she can't understand you or read you." So, I began to open the book more. I begin to study more, and God begin to show me that life is based on relationships and communication.

1 Corinthians 2:9 "But as it is written, eyes have not seen, nor ears heard, nor have entered into the heart of man, the things which God has prepared before for those who love Him."

*W*ow! That means that, like any love relationship, you have no clue what's in store if you don't give your all! Just imagine in return, if God told you what you're here for. Instead of dabbling and wondering, working here, trying this job or career, going to this school, being with this person and that person, but not knowing in full if this is the right decision? Well you won't know if you don't try right? According to scripture you haven't seen it yet, nor have you heard your best news yet. According to this scripture the formula is right there.... if you love Him! If you love Him, you will spend time knowing Him. In return you will receive Him!

There was a time where I was up doing great, then I would fall back down. Or when I experienced trauma in my life and sunk in a whole. Or when I dealt with a loss, whether it was losing my job, money, or a female. In my first marriage the daughter that I raised from birth, I found at years later that she wasn't mine. When she was 4 years old, I received the blood test saying that I was not the father and I lost it! At the time, I just was mourning over the fact that I lost my grandmother, and 2 years later my aunt that I was living back and forth with. I was very close to my grandmother and my Aunt, and that set me back like a computer in default mode. Because I was lost, I started to do everything from the past, expect cocaine. I felt as though God didn't love me. I used to ask myself all the time, "if He did love me why did He allow me to go through this and feel the pain during the process?". So, I went to drugs to medicate the pain, to numb it and try to drown my sorrows with liquor, but it made me angry and violent, and numb to other people's feelings. At that point in my life I became numb and dark. Which I should have known it would end up like that because on the liquor store it specifically says beer, wine and spirits, and those spirits definitely came! I could still hear God's voice trying to Father me, telling me which direction to go to again. If it wasn't for the accountability of others and for changing my environment, I would have become a statistic. You wouldn't have known my name, but maybe would've heard of me represented in a count as another number added to data for research that people wouldn't take into consideration. Then, I began to know the voice of God and began to be led by God and allow him to love me. I grew up in a home where there was no love and affection, so God connected me with loving and affectionate Pastors to break down walls that's been built. Now I'm able to break generational curses in my family by telling them I love them hugging my children and loving on my wife in front of them. That sets a Godly example of a true family. We are design to bring heaven on earth!

Poem
I Know Who I Am

Sometimes people will make you feel as though you're the black sheep or an outcast

Have you so focused on your failures where you're living in the past?

Every time you find peace you realize it gets robbed because misery likes company

The whole time God is saying let go and I will cause you to grow and come to Me

Instead of being free and searching for the key we beat ourselves up and confess the lies

While God is telling us, I made you in My image, you're not just here to get by

So, the next time someone tries to tear you down, call you out your name, say you won't amount to anything, don't bury your head in the sand

Stand firm, hold your head high, and boldly say not this time. I know who I am!!

Poem
Depression

Sometimes I wonder why the sky is blue

Sometimes people wonder why I do the things I do

I can't explain

That's like when you bleed, why is it followed by pain

Life has its own issues

Deep inside you feel misused

Surrounded by wet tissues

Go ahead end your life, no one will miss you.

Don't let Satan trick you!!

Praying to God for help

Your surrounded by people but your all by yourself

Feeling forsaken

Thoughts taken

Abused and mistaken; Time wasting

People hating, Lord what is this that I'm facing

I'm at the end of the road, end of the rope. What's the disguise of this blessing?

Lord if I don't receive anything else just remove this depression!

Chapter Eleven
Distractions vs Desires

Psalm 127:4 *"One thing have I desired of the Lord, that will I seek after"*

I always knew deep inside that I was different. I knew that I was going to be somebody. I always knew that greatness was inside me, I just didn't know what, so I just became myself. When you become yourself everything that belongs to you will be attracted to you. The issue is that it's very easy to look at others and dictate and judge your life based upon other views, and over what other people may think and we judge upon their success or values. So then we look at our past and our values and things that happened to us and we begin to be our own judge putting ourselves in the prison of our mind, not knowing the freedom that we possess. I never valued the importance of being alone or all one! In the book of Ecclesiastes, it says it's a season for everything. Before I found God, I truly believe from experience that because I didn't have faith or believe in God in my alone season, I didn't take advantage of being alone. Notice when your alone it's just you, your decisions, and your ability to achieve whatever goal. Your responsible for your own actions. You can study as long as you want, you can travel, you can be on what I call the road to discovery. Where we fail at is thinking that being alone is the same as being lonely. Lonely is a deep, emotion lacking intimacy and love. It's the pain that something is missing and can leave people feeling depressed.

If you're not careful you can get distracted and be put off course on the road to discovery in finding out why God created you. Like being distracted because you're consumed with who your soulmate is that he has prepared for you, that you miss your destiny or assignment on this earth. You can link up with the wrong relationship and you can go down. Or you can have the right relationship that can take you up. There's a quote I always say when I speak. Relationships are like elevators they can either take you up or take you down; you decide which floor you want to get off! I've been in relationships that I thought were good, but I didn't become whole and complete within. There were still some areas in my life that needed fixing that were fixed in the other person's life, but they were experiencing the same damage in me, but in a different form. The brokenness in me didn't fix anything, it was just breaking people around me, and I had no tools to fix the problem, so the problem multiplied. That's how people end up turning on each other, because of the fact people look at one another wanting the problem to be fixed with no tools and God is the carpenter. I'm talking about relationships, companionships and friendships. Notice the ending of each word it says ships because it takes you somewhere. It's easy for you to get together on common interest because of whatever your struggle or situation. You can easily find someone that's relatable and bam he or she is your drinking buddy or your partner to get high with. While somewhere down the line your desire got suffocated by life and you linked up with the wrong person and instead of holding you accountable, they compromise and begin to let you stay in your mess rather than challenge you. From that point the distractions become stronger! The voices of your distractions become louder and you became further away from your destiny. Guess what, I have great news! It's never too late to be great!!! I thought it was too late for me. I just turned 42 years and I'm like, Woah... I'm old, lol! But who would ever thought I'd go from selling drugs, smoking weed, cigarettes, acid, popping pills, alcohol, cocaine, being pronounced dead on arrival at the age of 19 years old, to now a National Gospel recording artist, an author, Speaker, Minister, Business owner of a Barbershop & Salon, Beauty Supply Company and now a Barber College!! Woah! Yeah, that's a lot! Oh, and last but not least, a Father of 6 beautiful wonderful children, and a Husband of 12 years to the most beautiful woman on the planet, Stephani Sturgis! My Queen! My desire for more in life was stronger than my distractions; and trust me, I had (and still have) distractions, but it was during my alone time with God where he led me and guided me!

My pastor has an acronym about Vices = Vicious Impulses that Cripples Effectiveness. If you ever used those vice grip pliers you know that once you have it there's no letting go, it's locked like a Pitbull. Well that's what a vice is. Like I said earlier I know people who own their own companies, homes, and had everything going for them, but linked up with a wrong individual who was hooked on drugs and sold everything, lost everything, and they began to be homeless, in and out of centers and prison because of the vice.

The devil has 3 avenues to grip you. Lust of the flesh, lust of the eyes, and the pride of life! (1 John 2:16) He uses different types of substance to grip you with that and from that we get entangled. Once I recognized that there was a grip on my life and the distractions that was in the way I chased after God like never before, and I'm free now! Over 20 years clean! Galatians 5:1 *"Stand fast in the liberty wherewith Christ hath made us free and be not entangled again with the yoke of Bondage!"*

Chapter Twelve
Live on Purpose

Proverbs 16:4 "*God made everything with a place and purpose; even the wicked are included-but for judgment.*"

Sometimes it's hard to believe that in the enormity of our entire Universe that God purposefully considered and planned out in detail every little thing. Within His great plan he gave every single creature, every living thing a Purpose. On the subject of purpose we have to define it accurately in order to get a clear understanding. Purpose defined is "Reason for existence". That is exactly what the writer of Proverbs 16:4 is saying, that everyone and everything God made has Purpose. God never created anything without significance.

I love the subject of Purpose because it's impossible to discuss Purpose without first discussing Significance. My Pastor Claude Bevier wrote a book called the blueprint and he talks about the main keys in life which helped me to get where I am today. He touches on significance. He began to share with me what the Lord spoke to him in a revelation. He said, "G-rod, the Lord began to minister to me. He said, 'I am going to tell you what significance means'. Then clear as ever He said, 'Significance is when you are so valuable that the world cannot function properly without your impact'". I was like "Wow, this was exactly what I needed to hear". I began to meditate on that for at least a month. The light came on and my journey became more clearer than ever. I now knew that chasing dreams, chasing money, chasing plans and intentions were not God's design.

I heard the late Dr. Myles Monroe say a profound statement and it was this, "The forest is not out in front of the seed, the forest is in the seed". See, what he was expressing in that statement was that everything the Seed needed to accomplish its Purpose or potential was already in the seed. The seed doesn't have to look outside of itself for any assistance to become a forest, it just has to be planted in the right environment and it will eventually become a Forest. I spoke on how key the environment was in previous chapters. Everything God created is in seed form. That's why Satan wants to cloud your mind with thoughts so you're not able to create. Just like that the chair your sitting on was once inside the trees.

So many people are in what I call, "The Hustle of Life". They get up every morning chasing after things they have to do and plans to carry out. They constantly look to get more and more money so they can survive, but the issue is that most of them get more and more but they are completely unsatisfied with life. As I stated earlier, Joyce Meyer speaks of this when she says, "It would be a shame for an individual to climb to the top of a large building and once they get to the top, they realize that they are on the wrong building". What a dissatisfaction it is to work and strive but never find fulfillment, the Bible calls this self-effort and toil. Just like the seed we discussed earlier, everything you and I need to be successful is already in us.

Also, in the book called the Blueprint which powerfully changed my life, my Pastor touched on the process of Becoming. The greatest act of an individual is the act of "Becoming" because once you truly Become, then and only then do you truly Belong. We all want to "fit in" we all want to be significant; we all want to know that our lives matter. That's important because when we die people won't remember us for how much wealth we've acquired or what kind of house we lived in, or what kind of cars we owned, they will only remember us by the value we added to others and the investment and impact we made to society. I went to a very close friend's funeral and a very wise friend of mine stated, "After it was all and done, we can say he was the man! He had the money, cars, women, neighborhood name, the flyest gear, was feared by many, but what value did he leave? After a couple months go by, the phone calls stop, the visitations end, and when the smoke clears what is he truly remembered by?" I was like, wow! Honestly, he really left his children nothing other than mourning and memories.

You have what it takes as long as there is air in your lungs and breath in your body you have to fight! Fight and never give up! Paul says to, "fight the good fight of faith". Why? Because in your daily walk you're going to have to fight something. Once you conquer one thing there's an enemy who's not happy with your efforts. He wants you to remain stuck but you gotta hold your ground until you make progress. You have to take one step at a time until you look back and see how far you came, which is the only time you should ever look back.

Today, lets agree in prayer for revelation, the uncovering of what already is. Let's pray that the Holy Spirit would remove the veil from our hearts to see what God has prepared for us, because we love him. Hidden in every person is God's original intention for their lives. So today we pray and agree for those things to be discovered.

Prayer

I know that I have a Purpose! I have a reason for existing! The Lord has made me absolutely significant. There is no one else in the universe like me. I declare that everything the Father has put in me will come out of me unhindered, unchecked by any opposing force. The Holy Spirit is daily uncovering, disclosing and revealing these things to me so that I can daily walk in them, in the Mighty Name of Jesus Christ. Amen!

Other Scriptures to Meditate on

Ecclesiastes 3:1 *"To everything there is a season, and a time to every purpose under the heaven"*

1 Corinthians 2:9, 10 *"But as it is written, Eye hath not seen, nor ear heard, neither have entered into the heart of man, the things which God hath prepared for them that love him. But God hath revealed them unto us by his Spirit: for the Spirit searcheth all things, yea, the deep things of God."*

Chapter Thirteen
I Made It

There's a formula I found out in life that was taught from my Pastor. This is the formula that I use in every area of my life! It's Intimacy, Identity and Destiny and its foundation is found in John 7:29. It says, I know Him (Intimacy) I am from Him (Identity) He have sent me (Destiny). That's my blueprint I follow in marriage, businesses, and relationships. I funnel everything through that, and I question everything through that. Am I spending intimate time with the Father? If not, then how will I know how I'm wired and what makes me fall into these traps and cycles? Lamentation says our Fathers have sin and they are not (deceased), and we've born their iniquities. You wonder why you have an urge to drink or use a certain substance or why you're promiscuous. It's because satan has followed your bloodline 2000 years ago to get you bound. My father was an alcoholic, his father was an alcoholic, and I became one with no desire. So, it's up to me to break the curse so it won't travel down to my sons. That's why a child can be living with his mother and father lives elsewhere and have never seen him but acts and does the same thing their father does. Men really don't live in intimacy, they don't like to be vulnerable, they don't like to be affectionate. We've been taught that's a sign of weakness, but I've lost so many loved ones and friends. I've seen so many lose their life to drugs so many incarcerated so many just lost their purpose in life as a whole, or just have no direction and not knowing what to do in life, and it puts a burden on me! I began to weep and share my feelings and be vulnerable and now I never thought living in a time like this I would see the world in the shape it is in.

We are in the last times, the last seconds. While I'm writing this, we are in the middle of a global pandemic with COVID19 that has swept throughout this world uncontrollably, where people so many are dying daily from it. I mean 4,591 died in one day, Woah! And it's still climbing! My desire to get the gospel out has been amplified to the fullest. So, it's very important to have a relationship with God now like never before. God's desire is for everyone to get intimate with Him so that they can know Him, and know who they are, so they can do their assignment. Their gifts, talents and abilities are what God will use to reach the lost, so they are able to come to the Kingdom of God. Your ability and skill are for you to share the gospel; the Good News! Aren't you tired of hearing bad news? Aren't you tired of experiencing the bottom of the barrel? You have been fearfully and wonderfully made! There isn't another you! You have been carved out created for such a time as this! Like I said before, it doesn't matter how you got here; according to Jeremiah Chapter 1, before you were formed in the belly God knew you. He sanctified you and set you apart. That's intimacy all over! He said He knows you. I'm a barber, I can cut your hair and God still will know how much hair I cut and whose it belongs to and also the amount left on your head. Do you think that he doesn't know about your problem and how to bring you out and give you direction? It wasn't until I got tired of trying to figure things out myself and doing things my way expecting different results but doing the same thing my way; until I gave it to God. Start praying! Regardless of what it looked like, I believed God, I got my expectations up. I put my trust on Him and then I start doing it His way. I then began to experience victory after victory! I now use my Gifts of rapping, drama, business, and speaking worldwide.

Chapter Fourteen
Victorious

As you are preparing to go to the next level in your life; whether its celebrating sobriety, recovering from a traumatizing experience in life, finding your purpose where you've laid down that dream or lost that passion... create a Personal Plan for your life! What is your mission statement? What you want to do in your life, when do you want to do it, and if you don't know pray until God reveal it. Think about something that frustrates you in this world that you wished was solved, or something out there that's a problem. Because normally, when things are a problem to you God has put it on your heart to fix it. Or it could be something small, not everyone is called to change the world, some are called to change your city, your community, your home, your bloodline, or your family.

Write down some personal goals that you want to work on for yourself. Jot down some things that you want to do differently in your life and start living life with a plan and goals. You have now gone through certain phases in this book of being lost but now found and probably didn't even realize it. While this is getting closer to the end of this book, it's the beginning of your destiny of your personal new journey of self-discovery. Everyday above the ground is a win! Subscribe to my website www.GerodSturgis.com to get notification on when my journal is ready so you can start working on living your destiny! You'll also be alerted when new music, materials and prayer confessions become available.

SECTION 3

DISCUSSION QUESTIONS

1. When did you realize the void you're trying to fill is God's love?

_____

_____

_____

_____

_____

2. Have you located yourself, or are you eager to get to your destination without proper direction?

_____

_____

_____

_____

_____

3. What makes you, you? Have you discovered the REAL you, not the "you" people think you are?

_____

_____

_____

_____

_____

4. What are some distractions that you face?

_____

_____

_____

_____

_____

SECTION 4
LOVE
REVEALED

Chapter Fifteen
What's Love Got to Do with It?

John 3:16 *"For God so loved the world that He gave His only begotten Son; that whosoever believeth in Him should not perish but have everlasting life."*

There is a famous singer by the name of Tina Turner who sang a song called, "What's Love Got to Do with It". I would say Love has everything to do with it! Fear is the root (or the tool) that satan uses to get his agenda done on the earth. Satan attacks our minds through intimidation, which paralyzes us and then isolates us and causes self-infliction or having us feel as if we're unworthy or not appreciated or loved. Notice it was during the time when we were at the weakest point; whether we just lost a job, bad relationship, financial problems having issues in our marriage problem with our children, health so on; which then pressures you to say the wrong thing: "I'll never get better, I'm always sick, I'll never get married, I'm always addicted, everyone in my family has this problem" etc. Life and death are in the power of the tongue and they that eat it enjoy the fruit thereof. What fruit? Life or death! So satan's way of placing fear in you isn't just in fear of this movie or my shadow or the dark. Fear is the very opposite of God's love; it's satin embodied.

So, let's talk about Love. I'm not talking the love that your thinking; that googly feeling, emotional love. Or that, 'I love you do you love me? Circle yes or no'. We're about to get to the root of why we fall into the snares of the enemy the way we do and get upset with people because we think it's them when it's really us who has a love deficiency. But if you don't know what true love is then you base your life upon people, places, and things that you put your expectations in and failed you because you put everything into it expecting a return on the level of passion but didn't receive it back and it caused you to retreat having the enemy to play with your mind. Do you ever give someone too much power mentally? You can't sleep or eat and stay bothered and they're somewhere living life, not even knowing that you're in the prison of your mind. If you mention their name you scurry, if you go to the grocery store and see their vehicle you go to another store, almost running out of gas just because you don't want to see that person. Go down a different aisle because you hear their voice or see them. Thinking everything they post is about you. That means you have given them power. It's really bad when you can't go to a location because it reminds you of them. Jesus said, "Father forgive them, for they know not what they do." Those were the last words before Jesus gave up the Ghost. Why? I'm glad you asked! Jesus defeated the cross but before He defeated it, He understood that His reason to be on earth was to redeem mankind. That God sent Him, which is the highest level of Love, giving. That's why it's better to give then receive. If you don't forgive your unable to receive. Jesus conquered every sin to mankind. When Judas betrayed Him, He could have easily held unforgiveness in his heart, but He told Judas go ahead and do what you need to do and do it fast. Jesus had to deal with forgiveness as the last thing because it is the hardest thing and the gateway to receive Love!

Matt 22:37-38 "*Jesus said to him, 'You shall love the Lord your God with all your heart, with all your soul, and with all your mind.' This is the first and great commandment. And the second is like it: 'You shall love your neighbor as yourself.'*"

If you are running into any disaster or shortage in your love walk it's because you're not loving God 100%. And if you're not loving God, then you're not loving your neighbor, and if you're not loving your neighbor, that means you're not loving yourself. It's called being selfish. We've all been there. I'm gonna take care of me, nobody loves me, cares for me, they don't visit me, see my pain, struggles etc. How am I going to eat, live, or survive? Not even going to mention the fact of trying to figure out what I'm here for. This person treats me like this; and so on. So, in the midst of all of that you try to form a relationship??? Thinking things will get better. Wherever you are, you are. When Adam was in the garden and he hid, he sewed fig leaves to cover himself. Out of that act mankind has been fighting the curse of covering. That's dangerous on any relationship level. Why? Because you then reflect what's on the inside out, and we wonder why our faith won't work. Another definition of reflection is seeing something original in another form or image.

When I come home from a long day of work and the tub is set filled with green alcohol or Epsom salt for my bones, lol, candles lit, soft waterfall music that my wife setup for me to relax, I love it! Then when I come into the room and see her dressed in sexy lingerie and smelling like Bath & Body Works, it's another romantic type of environment, if ya understand me. I would be a fool to talk about bills that are due and bring up past arguments and destroy that atmosphere with my flaws. I'd be missing out on the best of her love for me. I just receive it and let love take over and it then... envelopes. Now the same with God! He created the environment which is His Word, but if you don't know how much He loves you, and what He has set for you, and that He prepares a table in the presence of your enemies, that He has plans for you, then you will never receive His love.

Matthew 22:37 "*Jesus said to him, 'You shall love the Lord your God with all your heart, with all your soul, and with all your mind.' This is the first and great commandment. And the second is like it: 'You shall love your neighbor as yourself.'*"

Basically, God is saying, if you get these two things right, then you got them all right! Why? Because it's the seed! And inside the seed lies fruit or production. Everything comes out of love. The bible says love never fails. Love covers the multitude of sins. Not the fileo or eros type of love, but agape. I'll go more in depth on these types of love in the next section. But if you love you won't murder. If you love you won't cheat. If you love you won't commit adulteries, gossip, envy. Basically, God put it like this; if you ever take a test multiple choice and if you get these 2 rights, I'll give you credit for the other 98. Your failure does not cancel your assignment! Watch this because Abraham decided to leave his kinfolk and separate himself, even when he disobeyed by bringing lot. Abram became father of nations as far as his eyes could see. God released the blessing on him. Just get those two rigghhhhhtttttt!

1 Corinthians 13:2 *"If I have the gift of prophecy and know all mysteries and all knowledge; and if I have all faith, so as to remove mountains, but do not have love, I am nothing."*

This product comes with a warranty and guarantee, along with the manual which is the instructions in the bible. But we are so used to operating out of order and don't go back to the instructions until our life is out of order.

There is a warranty built within the guarantee. You know, like that card that slides out the box that says to mail in with your address. The manufacturer places that in there because they're more concerned about the product working to its fullest potential.

Fathers are more concerned about the child having a crib, and mothers decorating the bed, making sure everything is there that's needed before the child gets here. The baby doesn't come out the womb saying, "God, tell my Daddy to buy a crib and my mother to decorate my room and throw a baby shower before I get out or I'm not coming. No, out of love the parents do this and when the children are successful it's a reflection on the parent; it makes them look good. So, the warranty and guarantee is a reflection on the manufacturer. But a lot of times we don't mail that card with our address in. That card reconnects you with its source!! God is saying, "I want to Bless you, but I can't find you. I don't know your address!" Like Adam, he had an address, but he moved!! He hid from God and God went looking for him and said, "Adam where art though? You're making me look bad! Now mankind is going to think I don't love them, that I separated from them, that I'm the one that's causing these single mothers. That I'm the one that's causing these murders. Adam where art thou? What were you thinking? Who gave you these thoughts, this other system where you downloaded this information? Now you have to see a different side of my Love; the chastisement. Because of you they're going to blame me." So, you need to mail in the address so God can find you.

Jerimiah 29:11-13 AMP *"For I know the plans and thoughts that I have for you,' says the Lord, 'plans for peace and well-being and not for disaster, to give you a future and a hope. Then you will call on Me and you will come and pray to Me, and I will hear [your voice) and I will listen to you. Then (with a deep longing] you will seek Me and require Me [as a vital necessity) and (you will] find Me when you search for Me with all your heart."*

DEUTERONOMY 6:4-7 AMP *"Hear, O Israel! The Lord is our God, the Lord is one (the only God]! You shall love the Lord your God with all your heart and mind and with all your soul and with all your strength (your entire being). These words, which I am commanding you today, shall be (written) on your heart and mind. You shall teach them diligently to your children (impressing God's precepts on their minds and penetrating their hearts with His truths) and shall speak of them when you sit in your house and when you walk on the road and when you lie down and when you get up."*

Chapter Sixteen
Four Types of Love

This is where the breakdown of life begins. The bible says with all thine getting, get an understanding. Growing up I never knew about these different categories that I'm about to break down. Often times people tell you to go with the flow or go by what you feel. True Biblical, can I repeat, Biblical Love, doesn't mean that. Oftentimes people will say if it feels like love then it's love, well that's not accurate. What if it's lust? By no means am I teaching on marriage or relationships. I'm just giving you the difference of the two for the topic. Now love in its definition means an intense feeling or deep affection. Lust in its definition means very strong sexual desire. They both produce seemingly the same thing, and both give out the same signals and if you're not careful you will alter your path in life by chasing something that's a mirage. Now let's filter things through these four categories and see if we are out of order.

Storge

This is the family type of love. This is the type of love that you have for one another pertaining to your blood family. You don't have to work for this type of love or have to prove yourself like you would in (Phileo). This is the most common type of love. My children don't have to win my love, even though they try, because I love them just because I'm their Father. Just like you don't have to try to win the Heavenly Father's love. He loves you just because He's your Father. Its most natural! I'm a Father, naturally I'm going to love my children with no force. Its emotive or emotional knowing that my children were created through the acts of love brings a deep bond like no other. The type of love a mother has for her daughter, a type of love a father to his, and son, siblings to one another. This is what I was stating earlier. This is the family love. You can be familiar with one another and not really no one another. I lived with my siblings, joked, laughed, built memories, played sports, shared clothes and that love just grew as we got older to a bond. And some of my cousins became like siblings, that's how tight our love for one another was. But you can grow up in the same house and not even know someone. Still till this day there's certain things about me that can be familiar with about me (root word in family) but not know me. That's why I was able to be one character to the outside world but another person to my family. So, when I overdosed my parents never knew I did drugs. I was in the choir, church plays, always did what I was told in sports, went to work, and did everything perfect at my job. It caught everyone by surprise. There's a lot in you as well. Your family may not know the good or bad sides of you. This is the type of love where they say blood is thicker than water, not having the proper understanding you will carry this love into your view or ideal of what love is by receiving what you received from your family. Or your perception of love might be from the lens of your family and you can damage relationships based upon that principal and thinking that's what love means.

Phileo

This is a friendship type of love. Phillia, that's where we get the word Philadelphia, they call that the "City of Brotherly Love". You know why because the root word Philla is a friendship love.

This is the love felt between close friends, or mentor, classmates, teammates, and in between close knitted communities. This type of love of friends can turn to Storge, the family, were they're so close. It's not like eros, where it's passionate (we will explain that later) but it's more heartfelt and sincere; where you want to lessen their pain. If they suffer a loss sometimes, they have to just call their close friend up, the one who can understand more than their relative because they may not want to get judged of their pain and suffering momentarily. This is where they express their loyalty and express their victories as well as their valleys. I had one close friend and he saw me slipping. I went back to selling drugs, partying, doing drugs, making a couple of thousand here and there, making a name for myself somewhat. So, I come flashing telling him what I've been doing and what I've got like he hasn't heard. I was expecting him to give me props, like 'man you eating, you getting it'. He took me upstairs and told me, "What are you doing! This not you! You gave that life up! You have a family! What about your kids? What will they be in life if you don't get back with God?" And he reminded me of one of my songs I wrote when I was traveling the world. Then he said the scripture,

Luke 9:62 *"Jesus replied, 'No one who puts a hand to the plow and looks back is fit for service in the kingdom of God.'"*

I was blown away man, speechless! He could care less of what I've done. He just upper cut me with the *W*ord and I could have brushed it off thinking he was a hater and told him about what I was going through and let him agree with me and sugar coat and went on with my life. Or just accept it as a true friend who told me the truth to challenge me. Now that's brotherly love! If it wasn't for that moment of truth, I probably would be in that rat race street life juggling trying to live two different lives. But I'm grateful for the truth he gave me, and it helped me to be who I am today.

Eros

This is a passionate and intimate kind of Love.

If you translate this, it means sexual type of love where you get the modern term "Erotc" from. This is the type of love you feel for a lover. The pull of a beautiful well-dressed, sexy woman of your desire. The raw attraction does not know what lies within their inner soul. This is a dangerous type of love. This is basically the only type of love that when you hear the word love that you automatically are drawn to or have knowledge of thinking this is love. I like her, she likes me, and your life becomes altered and change because of it. So, you don't want to get close to a friend because you don't want them to think you love them with the eros and it could just be Phillia and a lot of times people crush the three together. I just read an article where a couple was getting fined because they had a baby and they were first cousins. That's because there's only one true love that all this stems out of and without properly appropriating it a lot of people get damaged and wounded all out of the name of love, and then you hear this statement: if this is Love then I don't want it! If you base your relationship just off of eros it will fail, no relationship can be based on sex only. And if your basing it upon that then I'm sorry to tell you that there will be a time when the sex stops. Then what? There's a deeper connection of love that's being ignored that they're seeking after. A void that no orgasm will fulfill. You would have to do what I say often when I counsel other couples. "Right now, your still in the air enjoying the ride eventually you will have to land the plane to avoid a crash." I never understood what true love was. I was lost so I figured using this type of love would be the answer. So, once I landed the plane and I didn't have anything concrete to give anyone. I left and I damaged more people than I could've imagined. It wasn't until I came to God where I realized what true love is. There are so many people that I speak with and counsel that had no clue what love was, let alone about these four types.

Agape

This is the highest form of love! Unconditional love, the God kind of love.

This love is birthed out of God the Father. It's the all-consuming love; Glory to God! This is the type of love that God has for his children; for you and I! This the type of love that held Jesus together when He died for us! This is the type of love that the Father redeemed us with and brought us back, paid the price, bankrupted heaven, sent his only son for a people that never knew Him. For some who don't want to know Him, but His love is so unconditional that He did it anyway. He wants everyone to have the chance to be found! I'm getting chills just writing this! This goes farther than the family love, the family bond only a few can understand this love. It is considered the greatest of the four. It holds no records of wrong, it's a reckless, selfless type of love. It's the type of love that will welcome a cheater, con, addict, hustler, robber, pedophile, rapist, liar, homosexual, racist; this type of love only sees love. Agape is to be free with no condemnation or unforgiveness. This type of love will create a standard for all other types of love to make you feel accepted, regardless of your flaws, weaknesses, blemishes, spots, bruises and scars.

Looking back at my Life and judging my life now I see where I dropped the ball. Again, it wasn't until I had a true encounter with God where he taught me to Love Him with all my heart all my soul, mind and love my neighbor likewise. I was wondering why I was being misunderstood. I was always trying to change people to get them understand me or love me. When I didn't see it I felt rejection and the abandonment and I see how the other three categories were toxic because I didn't know agape. So, I dealt with the depression and loneliness and started to party and be around people who I later realized was feeling the same emotions I felt. But they were covered up with alcohol and drugs and that will bring the worse out of people and a lot of relationships again was even ruined for from that. Thank God for his Agape love that I now have and practice on a daily basis.

Matt 22:37 *"Jesus said to him, "You shall love the Lord your God with all your heart, with all your soul, and with all your mind.' 38 This is the first and great commandment. And the second is like it: 'You shall love your neighbor as yourself."*

2 Corinthians 2:9-10 "*But as it is written: "Eye has not seen, nor ear heard, nor have entered into the heart of man the things which God has prepared for those who love Him. But God has revealed them to us through His Spirit. For the Spirit searches all things, yes, the deep things of God.*"

Poem
Drugs

"Friend"

"I destroy homes, tear families apart - take your children, and that's just the start.

I'm more costly than diamonds, more costly than gold - the sorrow I bring is a sight to behold.

And if you need me, remember I'm easily found.

I live all around you, in schools and in town.

I live with the rich, I live with the poor, I live down the street, and maybe next door.

My power is awesome - try me you'll see.

But if you do, you may never break free.

Just try me once and I might let you go, but try me twice, and I'll own your soul.

When I possess you, you'll steal and you'll lie.

You'll do what you have to just to get high.

The crimes you'll commit, for my narcotic charms, will be worth the pleasure you'll feel in your arms.

You'll lie to your mother; you'll steal from your dad.

When you see their tears, you should feel sad.

But you'll forget your morals and how you were raised.

I'll be your conscience; I'll teach you my ways.

I take kids from parents, and parents from kids, I turn people from God, and separate from friends.

I'll take everything from you, your looks and your pride, I'll be with you always, right by your side.

You'll give up everything - your family, your home, your friends, your money, then you'll be alone.

I'll take and I'll take, till you have nothing more to give.

When I'm finished with you, you'll be lucky to live.

If you try me be warned this is no game.

If given the chance, I'll drive you insane.

I'll ravish your body; I'll control your mind.

I'll own you completely; your soul will be mine.

The nightmares I'll give you while lying in bed.

The voices you'll hear from inside your head.

The sweats, the shakes, the visions you'll see.

I want you to know, these are all gifts from me.

But then it's too late, and you'll know in your heart, that you are mine, and we shall not part. You'll regret that you tried me, they always do.

But you came to me, not I to you.

You knew this would happen.

Many times, you were told, but you challenged my power, and chose to be bold.

You could have said no, and just walked away.

If you could live that day over, now what would you say?

I'll be your master; you will be my slave.

I'll even go with you, when you go to your grave.

Now that you have met me, what will you do?

Will you try me or not?

It's all up to you.

I can bring you more misery than words can tell.

Come take my hand, let me lead you to hell."

Signed

DRUG

Poem
Broken Silence

If I don't break the silence, then there goes the dreams

Then there goes the cure maybe for H.I.V

There goes the thoughts and desires bottled up blurry vision, I can't see

Now the heart turns cold Hard like concrete

Once proclaimed victory now I walk in defeat

If I don't break this silence

It may turn into murder/ burglar isn't that what's his name's kid I heard of the

Things they done on the news

I thought they had good parents, well apparently, they do

If I don't break this silence

Yes, we kiss, hold hands, make love, channel surf, Netflix, chill and watch sports

If I don't break this silence now, then I might break it at court

Divorce that is. This my property these my kids

Now the son is forced to be the head

Sister forced to be the mother no more childhood

I wished I knew the feeling of growing up being a kid

See, if I don't break this silence

I'll be stuck on this job getting minimum wage

People getting hired in and they get an increase of pay?

Well I guess that's ok. At least I'm still getting paid

Blind to the fact that I'm operating as a slave

Richest place on earth is when you take your dreams with you to the grave

If I don't break this silence, I could be another statistic

I got goals and dreams, they're out of my reach

I can't get it... Ahhhh forget it

If I don't break this silence

My temper will increase I'll be the home of grief, malice, rage, murder

From anger, awe nah, danger

My escape might become hate

Alcohol, sex, Percocet, Vicodin, weed, coke that's all I need

Because even though it's a tap for death how else will I be free

It takes me to a place where I can see.. maybe it's another trap

But if I don't break this silence then one day this silence will break me. I gotta speak!

Or should I just hold it all in? Where do I begin? I gotta break this silence; this silence is not my friend

But I gotta break it, I just can't take it, I'm tired of faking it

They said take one day at a time. But I just can't make it, I can't shake it, if I break it I might feel naked

Exposed but I don't know what to do, my hands I fold

I'm shivering I feel cold

But I gotta break this silence. I gotta feel free

Because if I don't break this silence it might be to late, and the silence might break me

Chapter Seventeen
My Purpose in Writing this Book

1 Samuel 10:6 "*The Spirit of the LORD will come powerfully upon you, and you will prophesy with them; and you will be changed into a different person.*" My purpose in write this book

As I scroll through my phone it seems almost daily there's an overdose. Me being a Gospel Rap artist even the more. There are so many influential people who've died in the industry over drug overdose, and so many more are fighting the addiction. My generation used to rap about selling drugs and lavish lifestyles, this new generation is glorifying using drugs. Which leaves it hard for this younger generation to advance because they are brought up in homes in which the majority are broken homes and they don't have any guidance because the parent is focused on providing and doing what's necessary to survive while the children are screaming for affection, love and attention. So, they look for it in sports but because there's no father figure in their home, they mistake correction or structure as being hard or judgmental and quit in that sport. Eventually the only thing at times that maybe keeping them in school would be sports or extracurricular activities but get dropped out then deeper emotions of failure are created so their native tongue will be the environment that they are custom to. Emotions like anger, bitterness, resentment, loneliness, fear, and then surround themselves with other like-minded individuals who suffer as well. How do they relate if they lack anything? Love, again! Love has plenty of faces! The main thing is that there's a void. My acronym for void is Vacuum One's Identity and Determination. So, they fill it up with a substance.

I remember when I used to perform or rap back in the day. I would get a pack of beer, a pint and a gram of weed and I would be in a zone. I used to be what they say "TURNT", turnt into another man. I would be in another zone listening to music and the lyrics would

86

come and I would feel unstoppable. A lot of the people I read about, and some I know personally, would use before they go out to perform; whether its strippers who try to get out of the zone of showing off their body and escape the reality of it. Or the entertainer trying to escape the fear of performance and the reaction of what the crowd may think about them. Or the comedian. But I find it going from a one-time getting high thing, to become a social thing to do at parties and clubs. Now a majority of these high-end elite entertainers you see on TV get exposed to addiction by starting off using socially where they used to control it, but now it controls them. I like how TI said in an interview, where he realized where it was getting out of hand and he turned that thing around. You would've never known the extent of his addiction due to his success, and now how he helps others out in so many ways. There are others who said that this is the only way they function; this is what brought them their success. Without it they wouldn't have it; they think it's what keeps them on top.

1 Corinthians 3:16-17 *"Know ye not that ye are the temple of God, and [that] the Spirit of God dwelleth in you? If any man defiles the temple of God, him shall God destroy; for the temple of God is holy, which [temple] ye are."*

A lot of times we blame God for some things, but when in all reality you damage your own body. Notice when Beyoncé gets on stage she turns into sasha fierce. You can see the change in Post Malone, Lil Wayne, 69; I can go on and on! A lot of rappers turn into another man. I get that you have to have a certain image and personality when you perform because it's entertainment, but when you rely on drugs to alter your mind you're engaging in witchcraft. I realized certain ways that I would act when under the influence, but again imagine being under the influence of the Holy Ghost: Glory to God!

When I gave my life to God and began to rap for him, I began to hear the voice of God. I would pray in the Holy Ghost and hear what God was speaking to me and said what He said. I began to prophesy on music! Before I was speaking curses and releasing curses. Now I'm speaking blessings and releasing blessings. The industry is flooded with addiction that we must continue to pray for. It's becoming a social drug at VIP private meetings, events, house parties and outings. With plenty of prayer and tools and resources My team and I have taken the challenge to put a dent into this. By me sharing my personal testimony and being an example, my prayer is that it will encourage others.

SECTION 4 DISCUSSION QUESTIONS

1. What is love in your own words?

   _____
   _____
   _____
   _____
   _____

2. Hurting people hurt people. By you not knowing who you are, how is it hurting others?

   _____
   _____
   _____
   _____
   _____

3. What are the four types of love?

   _____
   _____
   _____
   _____
   _____

4. How can you relate to the author of this book?

   _____
   _____
   _____
   _____
   _____

Notes

ROAD TO DISCOVERY WORKBOOK

CHAPTER 1

LOST MAY WAY

1. What causes you to be lost? And what steps are you taking to find your way?

_____

_____

_____

_____

_____

_____

_____

_____

_____

_____

_____

_____

_____

_____

_____

_____

_____

_____

_____

_____

_____

_____

_____

_____

_____

_____

_____

CHAPTER 2

DEAD ON ARRIVAL

1. Have you ever experienced, or came close to experiencing an overdose?

   _____

   _____

   _____

   _____

   _____

   _____

2. Did you keep on going periodically? If not, what made you stop?

   _____

   _____

   _____

   _____

   _____

   _____

3. Who did it effect?

   _____

   _____

   _____

   _____

   _____

   _____

CHAPTER 3

ABUSE

1. Abuse comes in many forms: drugs, sex, money, people.
    Explain what you were abusing and how you received help?

    _____
    _____
    _____
    _____
    _____
    _____
    _____
    _____
    _____
    _____
    _____
    _____
    _____
    _____
    _____
    _____
    _____
    _____
    _____

CHAPTER 4

HIDING

1. When you first got addicted who did you hide from and why?

_____

_____

_____

_____

_____

_____

2. How did people treat you once they knew?

_____

_____

_____

_____

_____

_____

CHAPTER 5

ACCOUNTABILITY

1. What does accountability mean to you?

   _____
   _____
   _____
   _____
   _____
   _____

2. Would you be further in your life if you had accountability
   sooner?

   _____
   _____
   _____
   _____
   _____
   _____

   Discovery: Link up with an accountability partner that will
   challenge you. Remember relationships are like elevators. They
   can take you up or down, you decide what floor you get off.

CHAPTER 6

RELATIONSHIPS

1. Name some relationships that have damaged you

_____
_____
_____
_____
_____
_____

2. Name some relationships that have built you up

_____
_____
_____
_____
_____
_____

3. Name some types of relationships that you want to have

_____
_____
_____
_____
_____
_____

Ditto Discovery from Chapter 5: Remember relationships are like elevators. They can take you up or down, you decide what floor you get off.

CHAPTER 7

WAKEUP CALL

---

1. What was your wakeup call?

    _____
    _____
    _____
    _____
    _____
    _____

2. List your call to action, and the steps for change

    _____
    _____
    _____
    _____
    _____
    _____

    Discovery: Find three scriptures to keep you anchored

    _____
    _____
    _____
    _____
    _____
    _____

CHAPTER 8

KNOWING THE FATHER

1. We all knew God as God, but not as Father. We think that God is this angry person with a hammer that every time we do wrong, He's ready to bang us. But he's a loving Father, ready to love us through all of our shortcomings to show us who we are nd give us love. Explain God's love as a Father and how you know Him as a Father.

_____

_____

_____

_____

_____

_____

_____

_____

_____

_____

_____

_____

Discovery: Find three scriptures where God reveals himself as Father

_____

_____

_____

_____

_____

_____

CHAPTER 9

GPS

1. A GPS system is unique in the fact that its voice activated, and you can put your destination in, but not before you locate yourself. The mind is the battlefield, the map to your destination. Locate yourself. Where are you?

_____

_____

_____

_____

_____

_____

_____

_____

_____

_____

_____

_____

Discovery: If you're not satisfied with where you are, then change it! You are in control of your own destiny. If people are causing you to fall then begin to cut people, places, and things out for 7 days or until a change takes place.

CHAPTER 10

KNOWING WHO I AM

1. Knowing who you are is the most important thing in your life, second to knowing the Father. How do you truly discover who you are?

_____

_____

_____

_____

_____

_____

_____

_____

_____

_____

_____

_____

Discovery: Find a quiet place to read God's Word and pray for God to reveal who you are as He did with Simon.

_____

_____

_____

_____

_____

_____

CHAPTER 11

DISTRACTION VS DESIRES

1. In your own words explain desires

   _____
   _____
   _____
   _____
   _____

2. In your own words explain distractions

   _____
   _____
   _____
   _____
   _____

3. How can your distractions affect you in finding your purpose in life?

   _____
   _____
   _____
   _____

   Discovery: Make a list of all of the distractions in your personal life, now make a list of your desires. Work on eliminating every distraction

   _____
   _____
   _____
   _____
   _____

CHAPTER 12

LIVE ON PURPOSE

1. Now that you realize you have purpose in life, what do you think your purpose in life is?

_____
_____
_____
_____
_____
_____
_____
_____
_____
_____
_____
_____
_____
_____
_____
_____

Discovery: Make a list of your habits, abilities, dreams, goals, and a problem that you have a desire to solve

_____
_____
_____
_____
_____
_____
_____
_____
_____
_____

CHAPTER 13

I MADE IT

1. By now you have made some progress on your path. If you're at this section, YOU MADE IT!! List some things that you've overcome in your journey thus far.

_____

_____

_____

_____

_____

_____

_____

_____

_____

_____

_____

_____

_____

_____

_____

Discovery: Read Jeremiah 1:5. Encourage others that you feel are losing hope. Remind them how far they are and obstacles that you overcame.

CHAPTER 14

VICTORIOUS

1. You are more than a conqueror! What are some things you are victorious over

_____

_____

_____

_____

_____

_____

_____

_____

_____

_____

_____

_____

_____

_____

_____

Discovery: List tools that will keep you living a victorious lifestyle.

_____

_____

_____

_____

_____

_____

CHAPTER 15

WHAT'S LOVE GOT TO DO WITH IT

1. It was love that brought us here, and love that takes us away. Name when you felt God's love to get you through a tough time

    _____
    _____
    _____
    _____
    _____

2. Name a time someone showed you love without judgement

    _____
    _____
    _____
    _____
    _____

    Discovery: Find in God's Word acts of God's love. Regardless of how you feel, show love towards someone you normally wouldn't show love to.

CHAPTER 16

FOUR TYPES OF LOVE

1. What are the four types of love

   _____

   _____

   _____

   _____

   _____

2. Explain what type of love you've been operating in the most, and why

   _____

   _____

   _____

   _____

   _____

CHAPTER 17

MY PURPOSE IN WRITING

1. You are on a road to discovery. Every step in your walk should lead to progress. What progress have you made from beginning to end?

_____

_____

_____

_____

_____

_____

_____

_____

_____

_____

_____

_____

_____

_____

_____

Discovery: Look back on your journal and read your own personal road to discovery

_____

_____

_____

_____

_____

_____

About the Author

Gerod Sturgis started his entrepreneurial journey landing a record deal as a national Gospel recording artist, who put out two stellar albums traveling a 50-city music tour that brought him to Adrian, MI, where he has been residing for the past 12 years. Since April '07 Gerod has been serving as a Minister at Restore World Church and doing music with Restore World Tour. He met and married his beautiful wife, Stephani, in 2008 and they have 6 amazing children.

In 2009, Gerod earned a Master Barber Stylist License and after working at a few shops, opened and ran Basilio Barbershop & Supply, successfully for five years. He made history as the first Black owned Barbershop in the city of Adrian, MI. In October 2020, Gerod successfully opened Legacy Barber College with full occupancy and a waiting list out to 2022. He made history in his city again, as not only the first Black owned Barber College, but the first Barber College ever to be established in the city and surrounding areas.

Gerod has helped countless people who have lost hope in life, to rediscover who they really are, and to find their God-given assignment in life. He has also recently launched two Non-Profit departments with A.C.T. International. One called Lost Now Found, that does music nationwide and ministers to the broken. The other is called Legacy Foundation, that takes donations to offer scholarships to promising students and applicants of Legacy Barber College that may have been incarcerated, or those suffering financial hardship. Both Non-Profits play major roles in giving back to the community in helping individuals to restructure and establish themselves in order to live life in purpose... on purpose!

Resources

<u>Lost Now Found Ministries</u>

We want to hear from you!

- Subscribe to our website and let us know how we can pray with you and believe God with you as you travel on your Road to Discovery.
- Get updates to your email about new music from G-Rod, and receive real-time notifications on new videos, prayer confessions, projects and more.
- Find out how to partner with our ministry with your monthly support and prayers, and how to volunteer to serve at LNF events.

www.GerodSturgis.com

Scan the code below to receive G-Rod's new single Lost Now Found.

Made in the USA
Columbia, SC
19 February 2023

12641178R00063